Tending to the Past

Reflections of an American History Teacher

To my family and friends—
the best things I know.

D1516483

Some of this book is fiction, some of it is fact.
But as Hemingway said, it's all true.

Tending to the Past
Reflections of an American History Teacher
Copyright © 2015 by Jim McGinnis
All rights reserved.
ISBN:1517561299
ISBN-13:978-1517561291

Acknowledgements

When this manuscript began to take shape, I entrusted four people with it. I owe a great debt of gratitude to Blythe Simmons Grossmann, Tamara Doehring, Michelle Atkinson Kuhn, and Jon Jordan. I can't tell you how difficult it was to give up that first draft for someone else's eyes. I am forever grateful to each of you for your guidance, advice, and tireless editing.

Thank you, Blythe for giving Jodi a voice. Thanks to all of you for helping me trust mine.

To Lloyd Soughers and Don Beggs for giving me the chance to be a teacher.

To Cathy Ford and Frank Merritt for making me want to be a good one.

To Bill Carey, Jim Lepper, Larry Ragsdale, and Jim Lewis for showing me how.

To my coach, Les Hall, who used baseball to teach me about the mysteries of manhood.

To Kay, my partner.

To my students...

Prologue

Francis Tiernan Quinn knew next to nothing of Lucille Clifton when he stumbled upon her poem. He was thumbing through an old literature text while waiting his turn on the copier, The room was actually a storage closet for the English department, and he warded off the claustrophobia by browsing through discontinued books. *I Am Accused of Tending to the Past* caught his eye. Three lines in, Clifton's verse reached off of the page and smacked him in the face. "I too stand accused of tending to the past," he said to himself. "Guilty is the plea." He closed the book and walked right out the door, forgetting completely about his copies.

Quinn's an old Floridian three decades into his profession, one point away from being graded a highly effective American History teacher. He loves America. He loves to talk about it; to read about it; to watch movies on it; even to listen to songs about it. He can wear you down. His passion and intensity, combined with occasional caffeine intoxication, makes his class a formidable experience. A day which begins with a touching memory or a Frost poem can quickly escalate into a raging, coffee-spilling, spit-flying tirade about the British and French mishandling of the Middle East. A lesson on the blind ambition driving America's move west can end with a tear-jerking story of Sam Houston's last words: "Texas, Texas, Margaret."

God, he loves it. And he's naive enough to get angry when others don't love it. Interrupting a story of FDR's first fireside chat isn't just rudeness, it's blasphemy. "American liberty," he repeats constantly, "is a religion." Of course, that leads to a digression about the statesmanship of Wendell Wilkie, who is credited with that quote. Heaven help the student who decides to check her phone messages during the lesson. "Would you do that in church?" Quinn asks, not waiting for an answer. But then there lies the contradictions. When his daughter strolls in with his grandbaby on her hip, everything stops. When a former student visits in his Marine uniform, everything stops...and begins again.

But these days, Quinn's all over the place; like a left handed pitcher who lost his release point. He has no control over his digressions and literary allusions. And he knows it. He dismisses it, not as a possible symptom of mental illness, but as the confluence of art and knowledge. Rationalizations are at times invaluable.

As a young teacher, he had been full of energy and emotion. He was fierce and spontaneous. He took risks, attacking his job with same tenacity he had when playing centerfield. But passion could only take him so far. He decided early on that he wanted to try to be a good teacher and thought it might help if he knew what the hell he was talking about. So he went back to school. And he began to take himself very seriously, insisting that students stop calling him "Coach." He was a teacher first, damn it.

He did become a good teacher. For a while. Everyone told him so. He was tough, gritty, and compassionate; still filled with youthful zeal. And through the early years he learned the most valuable of lessons — humility. He was blessed by being surrounded by seasoned colleagues, and he found himself open to their counsel. Of course, they were only too willing to offer it. There were those who saw in him what he didn't see in himself, and they became a great support system. His drive was tempered by respect for those he aspired to follow.

> *I am only a teacher. Ten or twelve years ago, I stumbled upon a Jim Harrison interview that led me to that realization. He said, "I learned that I can maintain my sense of sacredness of existence only by understanding my limitations and losing my self-importance." If I am only a doctor, carpenter, engineer, police officer, preacher, congressman; "it promotes the humility needed to function as a human being." I am only a teacher. —F. Quinn*

Through the years he became popular; liked; respected. Approval from students and peers was validation. The problem with that of course is that we humans often confuse good and popular. One is not necessarily the other. Quinn got lazy. He forgot his humility lesson. As the years rolled on, like the lawnmower in his garage, he rested on his laurels... The "Mr." gradually disappeared and he became known simply as 'Quinn.' (It seemed that students took him far less seriously than he did himself). Somehow he slipped from a source of respect and admiration to one of local amusement. Somewhere along the way things changed. One by one his mentors retired. He battled the limitations of parenthood. He drank too much. And he ran head on into a deadfall of education reforms. And oh yeah, he got older. No longer was he the Young Turk.

Quinn drifted through his fifties. The realization that he was no longer the sage on the stage was a bit troubling to him, but he hid it well. He had been a popular teacher. The time had come for him to try to become a good one again. But in the wake of a new order in the profession, he wasn't sure he could get there from here. Humility had yet another lesson to teach him.

It seems it's not enough anymore to be passionate and knowledgeable. It's not enough to be devoted to your students. Frank Quinn is indeed an endangered species, moving ever closer to extinction. Sadly, he doesn't even know how close he is to the end of things. He's now in the sunset of his career, not because he's burned out, too old, or bored. He's on his way out because the tide of change keeps pulling him farther out to sea. The rules have changed. The onslaught of cookie-cutter reforms have rendered his profession ungraceful, to borrow from the poet. When once he saw his later years in the classroom as a harvest, they had now become a winter.

Then he decided to write this book.

October 10

Ray Donohue stuck his head in the door. Quinn was sitting at his desk with his feet propped up, Tom Petty singing in the background.

"What are you doing?" Ray asked. "The day's over."

"Reading Howard Beale quotes, Ray, what's up?"

"Who the hell is Howard Beale?" Forty years in Florida took nothing from Ray's piercing Long Island tone.

"Come on, you remember the crazy anchorman in *Network*. Peter Finch played him." Quinn started to read a line out loud but stopped mid-sentence. His friend didn't seem all that interested.

"You shouldn't have quit coaching, Frank," Ray said, shaking his head. "You'll go friggin' crazy."

"Hell, I'm already there."

"You never answered me this morning, can you make it to *Meg's* for one or two? I still have one of those gift cards they gave us." Both men were well known around Melbourne's only Irish pub…one of the owners' sons played for them years ago and he always took care of the old ball coaches.

"Sure, what time?" It had been a while since the two of them had met for a 'coaches meeting.'

"Will 4:30 work?" Ray asked. "I've got a few errands to run."

"Four o'clock it is."

Ray left to run his errands and Frank Quinn returned to his quotes from the Mad Prophet of the Airwaves.

> All I know is that first you've got to get mad…things
> have got to change, but first you've got to get mad.
> –Howard Beale

He had caught the end of the old movie the other night and wanted to revisit Finch's character, but the chance to sit down and shoot the bull with an old friend was far more attractive. He closed up his room and headed downstairs.

Quinn's link to Melbourne High School went far beyond his thirty years of teaching. It was part of him. Thirty five members of his family had graduated from Mel-High, but he was not among them. He and his oldest sister went to Satellite High when his parents were renting a house on the beach. Quinn fell in love with two things at Satellite—baseball and a beautiful blonde named Jean. Baseball seduced him but Jean wouldn't even give him the time of day. He would not give up.

He played centerfield for a rather taciturn West Virginian who kept him on the straight and narrow during a turbulent time. War interrupted both his education and his baseball career. They sent him off to Vietnam, as the song goes, on his senior trip.

Quinn survived, came home, and went back to school; heading north to Gainesville and earning a degree from the University of Florida. He never got Jean out of his head, and after a long courtship, they married and settled in old Melbourne. Being a veteran was no help getting a job, so Quinn paid the bills by working construction and covering high school sports for the local newspaper.

He spent several years framing houses in Satellite Beach and became fairly competent with a hammer, but he never lost his obsession with baseball. The game had treated him very well through the years. Baseball kept him focused when nothing else would. Quinn felt he owed something to the game and longed to be part of it again. He took a side job coaching the JV baseball team at Melbourne, and it just so happened that the principal's son played on that team. It became a very valuable connection. A year later, Quinn was given the opportunity to coach on a full time basis. Again, baseball rewarded him with the chance to do what Quinn came to believe he was put on the Earth to do—teach.

Like Conroy, he believed that sports was a language of love between men who could never figure out how to communicate otherwise. When all else failed, he and his father, or he and his son could connect through baseball, football, and basketball.

Frank was halfway through his Guinness when Ray got to the pub. He grabbed the stool beside him and bellied up to the bar. "So Francis, what are you doing with yourself?"

"Uh, hanging out with the dogs and granddaughters," Quinn replied. "Writing a book. Working on the boat."

"A book?" Ray laughed. "Oh my God, Quinn, you've always been full of shit!"

"Finished?"

"Hell, no. Not even close." Frank knew what the reaction would be. With Ray Donohue, there was always levity.

"Can I read it?" he asked.

"I don't know. When I'm done, I guess."

"Am I in it?" Ray asked. Quinn just smiled and took a drink.

"Well if I'm in it, I should get a preview." Ray was wound up today.

"I don't think it works that way," Quinn responded.

"What's it about?"

"What do you think, asshole? It's about teaching… teaching American History. Twain said write what you know. That's what I know. Pretty much all that I know."

Ray checked his phone and took a drink of beer. "Sounds riveting."

They ordered another round and let the conversation drift to baseball and family stuff. Ray took the remaining portion of his beer and carefully poured it into the new bottle. Quinn never figured out why he always did that, but was never curious enough to ask.

"So, this book you're writing, a bunch of rants about what's wrong with public education?"

"Partly, yeah," Quinn answered. "But a lot of it deals with the good stuff."

"That's gonna be a damn short book, Coach."

Quinn leaned back on his barstool.

"Why don't you get your ass back in the dugout with me, where you belong?" Ray said.

Quinn laughed. He knew Ray would much rather his old hitting coach be back in the dugout with him, instead of having him going off on this new 'pursuit.' But something had changed about Quinn. He was done with coaching, at least for now.

The two had been coaching and teaching together for the better part of thirty years, and they had an absolute blast doing so. The trust between them was unbreakable. Although they were quite different in many ways, there was a connection that transcended baseball. Francis Quinn had no better friend. Ray had a way of tempering Quinn's seriousness, usually with biting sarcasm. He was always there, keeping Quinn's feet on the ground.

"I wanted to write a book about the good stuff, Ray, I want someone…anyone to know that there is a lot of good in the old ways."

"So I am in the book," Ray said, laughing.

"Yeah, a little. I changed your name." Ray about choked on his beer.

"And I can't read it till it's done?"

"It won't make any sense."

"Ha!" Ray laughed again. "It won't make any friggin' sense anyway!"

"It's sort of a collection of essays. Not even sure what order they're going in."

"Well, I can't wait," Ray said dryly.

They finished their beers, paid their tab, and headed out.

The next day Quinn sent a student down to Ray's room with a manila folder. "This is real important, Amanda, make sure this gets in Mr. Donohue's hand."

Preface

I am accused of tending to the past
as if I made it,
as if I sculpted it
with my own hands. I did not.
-Lucille Clifton

Following Lincoln's advice, I've spent many years writing down my thoughts and then throwing them in the fireplace. This collection is what somehow survived. These writings lie at the heart of who I am and what I've been trying to do over the years. Some come right from conversations I've had with students — lectures, poems, sermons, and rants. Others are products of my own experiences, what I've seen and heard, and things I've come up with late at night or early in the morning.

This compilation may not be what you expect. You may well close this book and put it down quickly. But I'm hoping you'll pick it up again. It's about history...American History...teaching American History. And it's also about me. As far as the history stuff, much of what I've got to say is not new, but reminders of things we may have forgotten — willfully or accidentally. There are essentials that need to be taught, right now. There are things that need to be said over and over again.

I've spent much of my adult life learning about and teaching about America, in all its tangled complexity — its power, its generosity, its recklessness, its incoherence and spontaneity. And to borrow from the poet, the laughter all mixed up with the serious stuff. I have tried to see my country with both eyes open, so to speak; the conquests, betrayals, and incredible achievements. Through all of it, I've tried to comprehend the gift we've given the world.

And what is this America? Frost said it's hard to see, from within or without. Why do you suppose that is? Oftentimes, we see it in bits and pieces in the rearview mirror as we go speeding by. *Oh, that's America.* Who are we, anyway? At times, we seem to be a mere collection of splintered enclaves. Other times, we appear to be like Wynton Marsalis' New Orleans — a place with diverse ethnic groups "stewed into a...musky bowl of gumbo."[1] We don't always like each other, trust each other, or treat each other fairly. But here we are, as the jazzman would say, improvising.

And what does *unAmerican* mean? That word comes out of my mouth on a frequent basis. What other cultures wrestle with such a concept? I'm not sure I can define it, but like the Supreme Court's explanation of obscenity, I know it when I see it.

There have been times through the years when former students have come up to me and said things like, *"I loved your class. I'm not sure I liked the American History stuff, but I sure liked your stories. When you would talk about your family or growing up in Florida, I really enjoyed that."* I can't tell you how gratifying that is to hear; how rewarding it is to receive such validation. But folks, that is the American History stuff. It is the range of human life—the beauty and ugliness; the city and the country; the haves and the have-not's; the happy and the sad; the missionary and the drunk; the visionary and the fool.

In our efforts to comprehend America, there's an urge to try to boil it down—to pin it down and reduce it to its simplest terms. Try as we may, we can't do it, for if indeed this nation is an experiment with human nature, how can we ever simplify that? What needs to be boiled down is the very meaning of America. Jefferson's proposition is sewn into the fabric of our society. The American Idea—the belief in human liberty and equality as the foundation for a country—should always be the centerpiece of any discussion of life in America. The Idea permeates not only the examinations of our economic and political development, but also the culture. Especially the culture. The literature, the art, and the music are all interwoven in this American Idea. Louis Armstrong can teach us about this nation, as well as Thomas Edison and Bill Gates. The radical notions of freedom and equality are manifested in the drama and creative tensions of American life.

If you look at events around the world today, or right here at home for that matter, democracy is either on the run or on the rise.

---

[1] Wynton Marsalis. "Saving America's Soul Kitchen," TIME Magazine, September 12, 2005 Vol. 166 No. 11:

Never has it been more important to look at it, digest it, and understand it; not just from a political perspective but also a social one. In loving this country and holding hopes for its future, I believe our history holds a special significance.

Nevertheless, American History is being marginalized. We live in the culture of planned obsolescence. And as we lose the emphasis on history, we lose the rootedness of the human condition. By being taught no history, the individual acquires the general impression that the past is not important; the old ways of doing things are obsolete; anachronistic. That impression is dangerously false. There may well be conventional methods that are ineffective, but it's not because they are old.

By teaching no history, a society is saying, *"nothing done before matters."* And by constructing a curriculum and implementing teaching methods and standards that ignore what has worked in the past, schools are saying, *"nothing done before matters."* Surely there are some exciting new ideas out there, but that doesn't mean that the old ideas can't be just as effective and exciting.

I stand here, waist-deep in my own failings. Teaching is such a daunting endeavor. To be anything but humble would be proof positive that I'm delusional. To profess to be an expert would confirm suspicions that I have long since lost touch. *I am not blind to my shortcomings.* But Twain said write what you know and I know a little about teaching kids and a little more about America.

As I will say all too often before I'm through, I'm not sure what makes an effective teacher. There is more than one way of doing things. There have been times when I failed miserably. I've been earnestly boring, so much so that I could hear my own voice. I have been wrongfully swayed by majorities and grossly misled by mavericks. I've stood at the door and apologized to my students for lousy lessons. But I do know a few things. I know that a teacher must be willing to take chances; to take the risk of boring his students; to gamble on *not* reaching them—on going over their heads. He must be willing to fail…to fall flat on his face, and then pick himself up, dust himself off, and then climb right back in.

So these are the thoughts, musings, and passages from the ragged but ever growing collection of an old Floridian. I have been known on occasion to rant; mostly about the countless education reforms which are often thinly disguised recycled failures of the past. It's easier to criticize public education than to offer up viable solutions. But when the curriculum moves further and further away from the foundation, when we seem bound and determined to try to fix what's not broken, it becomes necessary to speak up.

This is not just a bunch of parting shots; actually, I hope I have some miles to go before I sleep. I do love teaching. So for the most part, I will try to spare you the "scathing indictments," and keep my moral outrage at bay.

But I won't make any promises.

The Value of History

Why study History? ...the inescapable question

with apologies to Aldous Huxley:

"...You all remember," Said the Controller, in his strong deep voice, "you all remember, I suppose, that beautiful and inspired saying: History is bunk." "History," he repeated slowly, "is bunk." He waved his hand; and it was as though, with an invisible feather whisk, he had brushed away a little dust, and the dust was Thomas Paine, Roger Williams and Walt Whitman; some spider-webs, and they were Ft. McHenry and Walden and Birmingham. Whisk. Whisk — and where was Henry Clay, where was Frederick Douglass, where were Sam Houston, Alice Paul, and Daniel Webster? Whisk — and those specks of antique dirt called Saratoga, Normandy, and Gettysburg — all were gone. Whisk — the place where Jamestown had been was empty. Whisk, the cathedrals; whisk, whisk, Lincoln and the Thoughts of Jefferson. Whisk, Passion; whisk Requiem; whisk, Symphony; whisk... "That's why you're taught no history," the Controller was saying.

Why then is it so important to study our history? I don't think we ask that question enough. And if we do ask it, we sure as hell don't try hard enough to answer it. It should be asked every day. For many, it begins and ends with that patented social science response: "we must learn from past mistakes." How's that one grab you? It's certainly valid, but it falls short. It's too simple. "No story is a straight line, Pat Conroy said. "The geometry of a human life is too imperfect and complex." Surely, the value of history and the reasons for knowing it are as varied and complicated as human nature itself. And well they should be. In this society, we've developed the nasty habit of trying to make complex things simple and simple things complex.

If the only legitimate reason to study the past is the age old political application of cause and effect, I think we're in trouble. In our quest to find meanings of the past, we just might overwhelm ourselves with all of the theories on the broad historical significance of events. Serendipity has its place. History is filled with ironic twists and unintended outcomes. So then, the story of this great experiment with freedom can't simply be told from the top down. To be understood; to be appreciated; to be of value; the story must be told from every conceivable angle.

To be sure, we do hope to learn from our mistakes, and to use our experiences as guides for future decision-making. It's important that the French know which way the Germans are coming. America itself took that ominous path into Afghanistan, following the Persians, the British, and the Russians. But the value of history manifests itself in many other ways. Just as the individual is constituted by his or her past, so is the community; and the nation.

Not only do we need to learn political and economic lessons, we also need the past to build connections to each other and within ourselves. We need history to give us a sense of place. It gives us examples of character and virtues that help us lead our lives. The past struggles of men and women can show us how to live, and how not to live, for that matter. History teaches us about people who lived responsible, courageous, interesting lives. Of course, there are plenty of cheaters and scoundrels and buffoons to talk about also. In the unique case of America—a nation built upon the idea of individual freedom and equality—we are drawn to the stories of men and women who expressed, defended, or furthered "the Idea," for it defines us as individuals and connects us to our civilization. It's the pioneer finding his way through the wilderness; the musician finding his own sound; the woman sitting down when the world kept telling her to get up.

Men and women of history are terribly flawed, but they have achieved extraordinary things. In understanding their stories we can better understand ourselves, and realize that each of us may well be capable of good and great achievements.

We need to remember. For the sake of remembering. Reading or hearing about someone with memory loss makes me shudder. A great fear I share with millions of aging humans is the prospect of my body outliving my mind. It's terrifying. Amnesia leaves a person floating without any connection to anyone or anything. He lives on with a blank slate: no successes or failures; no relationships; no birthdays or Christmases; nothing. Christopher Hitchens put me on to this. He was troubled by phrases such as *make a new start* or *born again*: "Do those who talk this way truly wish the slate to be wiped?"[2]

Hitchens went on to say that when we lose someone that is close to us, part of the grief lies in the loss of a person who knew us. Losing a loved one takes some of you with him. He knew your humor; your moods; your strengths and weaknesses; your fidelities and flaws. He is gone, and he took part of you. When we forget— when we lose a part of our past—we lose a part of ourselves. And so it is with nations. In our society today, we find the disturbing symptom of *collective amnesia.*

The political pressure to show empirical gains in learning has contributed to educators relegating history to the outer edges. The cost of marginalizing American History in our curriculum has played a part in the estrangement of history from our culture. This is no small event. Once we are separated from the ideas of the Revolution, the core begins to erode, and we are cut off from who we are.

We are all products of everything that has happened to us up to this point. We are who we are because of; in spite of; and for the grace of; our past. Along with the strands of DNA, each of us has been shaped by our own personal, cultural, and national histories.

Remembering is no easy road to travel. The price we pay is nearly as high as the cost of forgetting. I was reading about the "ethnic cleansing" that took place in the Balkans during the 1990's. Soldiers interviewed talked of visiting vengeance upon the grandchildren of those who had wronged their grandparents. Could that possibly happen here in America? I doubt it. This is not to say we are in any way morally superior. It's just we can't remember what we did last Thursday, let alone pass down a grudge through generations. There's something refreshing about that, but also very discomforting. What else are we forgetting?

There are young people of color today who walk around with a vague sense of anger, and many don't even know why. It's rooted

---

[2] Christopher Hitchens, *Hitch 22, A Memoir (New York: Twelve/Grand Central Publishing, 2010), 367.*

in something far deeper than police profiling and the cycle of poverty. They are detached from the civil rights movement because they have no historical recollection of the long fight for justice. The outrage expressed by modern activists rings strangely hollow perhaps because they too are disconnected from the stream of American History. People without a personal sense of history cannot see themselves as a link in the chain. If a young woman really knew the story of Alice Paul, how could she not make the effort to vote?

On the other hand, many other Americans are strangely insensitive to the rights of others because they too have been cut off from the narrative. When we do take the time to learn, we are often guilty of taking historical events out of context, which skews our understanding of the events and the characters involved. We just "drop in" to the story, making no effort to grasp the complexity of circumstances.

History is at the core of an individual's identity, and it is the glue of a friendship, a community, and ultimately a nation. We build what Robert Bellah called "communities of memory."[3]

The connections we make can also tie us to *place.* Creating a sense of belonging to a part of the natural world can give us an identity. As a native Floridian—where it seems that everyone is from somewhere else—I've often witnessed among my neighbors a lack of sense of place. In Wallace Stegner's explanation of "place," we discover another valuable role for history.

The knowledge of place grows out of working, investing, sacrificing, and of course, telling the stories of those experiences, whether they be times of prosperity or catastrophe.[4] Each individual must sweat and bleed for himself, but the stories, now, they can draw him in to something deeper.

In Stegner, we're reminded of how deeply personal our history can be. World War II takes on a whole new meaning when one discovers her great grandfather fought in it. The Great Depression

---

[3] Robert Bellah, *Habits of the Heart, Individualism and Commitment in American Life* (Berkley: University of California Press, 1985), 153.
[4] Wallace Stegner. *The Sense of Place (New York:* Random House, Inc., 1992), 2.

becomes much more powerful when she finds out her grandparents lived through it.

Still, education reform seems more focused on producing reliable employees than responsible citizens. In a democratic society, history has a great functional value to its citizens. Just as Luther "suggested" to the Church that it reach back to its roots, America would do well to reconnect with its founding. I believe that starts with how we teach American History. We need to teach more of it, especially the beginnings. The words of Jefferson and Paine are as new and fresh as the morning. Near the end of the movie, *Field of Dreams,* James Earl Jones gives a stirring soliloquy. He describes America as a place that steamrolls over its past again and again. I concur, but the secret to finding the meaning and purpose of this republic can't be found in reinventing America, but in rediscovering it.

I once heard a colleague say, "If a teacher didn't believe that his course was the most important subject in the curriculum, he's probably not worth a damn anyway." Of course, we know the strength and beauty of an education lies in its depth and breadth. But I'll tell you, because America has such a unique place in civilization, American History should hold a unique place in our education. Citizens have a responsibility to understand the American story. Furthermore, we have an obligation to pass that story on. So, in essence, teaching and learning American History is (intrinsically) tied to duty, and if we don't teach it in its entirety, we are shirking that duty. There, I said it.

Our lack of understanding of the meaning of America puts us in great jeopardy. We are vulnerable because we allow ourselves to be informed only by those driven by a political agenda. It's astonishing to hear pundits play upon our basic ignorance of the founding principles. It is nothing short of disgusting to hear talking heads (from both the left and the right) misrepresent our Founders, or worse yet, take them out of context.

In talking about America, there is a noble impulse to try to say something new, something profound. But you know, once you get past the Founders; and Lincoln, Emerson, Thoreau, maybe John Muir; there isn't a whole lot left to say that hasn't been said before. The trouble is we keep trying. Experiences can be unique and profound but the Idea is one and the same. We burn a hell of a lot of time and energy attempting to "explain" America with a fresh, new perspective. Textbooks are filled with human interest stories of success and triumphs over injustice and hardship. This is all well and good, but they lack the fundamental connection to American values and principles. The best explanations are right here in plain sight already. Unfortunately, we sacrifice precious time that should have spent learning about the bedrock principles established by Hamilton, Madison, Adams, and their contemporaries.

The young mind is naturally resistant to looking backwards, but that's okay, it's alright. Learning American History can be a painstaking process. But let's not water it down or thicken it up just to make it easier to digest! JFK reminded us that Americans do things not because they are easy, but because they are hard. The Founders spoke in present tense. They knew their own shortcomings, but they embraced a notion of the expansive nature of liberty and equality. If we don't establish that concept by teaching the beginnings, how can we hope to instill in students a perception of expanding freedom and justice?

We need to make relevant the vision — to make sense of the Idea in the modern world. But we have to teach it before we can do that! Abraham Lincoln spent much of his time *reminding* his audience of what they already knew: Jefferson's words. Many in his audiences had no formal education, but they knew things. He built upon their foundation of knowledge. But if we don't establish among students a knowledge and understanding of our founding principles, how can we build upon them? How can a student fully appreciate the power of Martin Luther King's message if he does not know the connection between King and Lincoln and Jefferson? Unfortunately, we often take shortcuts and speak of wisdom severed from its original context. In our haste, we love to raid the coffers — to pick and choose the words of the Founders to suit our designs. The danger is that we gradually cut ourselves off from the founding principles, and the truth loses its real meaning.

Use our Founding Fathers' quotes;
Still good for a couple hundred thousand votes
From those who visited Monticello once
And admired all the quirks and stunts.

But there's more than gadgets up there on that hill
I heard a man of prominence declare,
"It's a monument to human will."
He's got plenty of ideas to which he never did lay claim
Even then, he'd gladly share,
 For you really can't discover or invent
what's not already there.

In the mystery of Jefferson
We find the mystery of America
Waiting to be thought about and talked about!
For in each of us we find
Our hope and faith all tangled up
and intertwined with doubt;*
Giving us humility and strength
To ponder things in depth at length

America may be more than the collective wisdom of the Founders, but that is to say that the house is more than the foundation. Sure, it's more, but it isn't less. It sure as hell isn't less. Learning about the character of George Washington is just as valuable today as it was 150 years ago. It's difficult to decide what to leave in and what to leave out of a high school history course. We can argue over many items (Again, I don't want to leave anything out), but there can be no debate over whether we should teach Jefferson and Lincoln.

There is a force afoot in our culture to eliminate anything considered remotely offensive or discomforting. We teach like we're walking on eggshells, so frightened to be provocative or controversial. We sanitize the material and smooth the edges to the point of making a useless product.

As I said before, our history is riddled with flawed individuals—people like you and me, as Clay Travis said, "struggling to be better than they are." The stories offer us hope and move us toward the better angels of our own nature. If we remove everything that is offensive or upsetting, we are guilty of doing what totalitarian regimes do—cleansing history of all that conflicts with our agendas.

In barbershops; at bus stops;
And exchanges over countertops.
What we stumble on in pubs
Or 'round the kitchen table;
Without doctrine. Without party. Without label.
The free market of the mind
Challenges the orthodox, leaving certitude behind!

My opinions change, and they should. The American democratic tradition is rooted not only in the expression of one's views, but also in listening to others'. For me, a seven-word sentence captures the spirit of liberty: *I never thought of it that way.*

Opinions should change. Principles should not. That said, before anything else, we have a responsibility to first understand those principles—the whole and genuine nature of them. Again, I say to rely on politicians and pundits to school us on the Founders' values, ideas, and motives is to shirk the duty of citizenship. A teacher has to stay true to those principles.

American History is the story of this ongoing experiment with individual freedom. How can anything be more important? Any lesson in Science; in Math; in English; must be rooted in what Emerson called the sacredness of the individual mind. Give students information and let them—make them—think for themselves. No lesson goes anywhere without it. That, is the American Idea.

These are contentious political times, and our inability or unwillingness to sit down and find middle ground is proof that we're disconnected from the principles we profess to love. Surely, I have my own political views, and some of my closest friends passionately disagree with me on many issues. We get along, but I know many people who will go to great lengths to steer clear of any political conversations.

What are the two possible results of having a political debate? It will either bolster your views; or heaven help you, it may influence you to change your opinions. But it should not be risky to relationships to discuss, debate, and argue politics. Hell, the seeds of the Revolution were sown in a Boston tavern! The very essence of democracy requires the free exchange of ideas—not merely between our leaders, but also among citizens.

October 12

The weekend brought a breeze to central Florida and a relief from the stifling humidity. Temperatures plummeted to the mid 60's and the natives were thrilled. They took it as a change of seasons, and on this Sunday morning, Quinn stood out on the old wood deck in his shorts and flip flops sipping coffee. The dogs were all fed, and they roamed the backyard as morning broke. A feral cat or two had apparently taken up residence in the woods behind the house, and Donegan, the Chocolate Lab, felt obligated to announce his presence to them. Meanwhile, Shadow, the young female wandered blissfully around the yard.

Quinn stood by the rail and read over what he'd written the night before. Shaking his head, he remembered Hemingway's line about the first draft of everything being shit…as was the second and third, or so it seemed in this case. He never wanted this thing to become a book of rants. He had done enough of that in his time, forgetting substance and replacing it with what a colleague once called "bombastic, invective-laced moral outrage." She was obviously an English teacher, but the barrage had done its job. Quinn got the message. He had grown to dislike the tone of his own righteous indignation.

He wanted to show how teaching looked through the narrowed glimpse of an old romantic. He had learned to squint, as Harrison said, "to see love among the ruins," and he needed to write about all that was good about the classroom…or at least what he knew of it. Years ago, Quinn had made up his mind to wall himself off from the maddening bureaucracy and to seize the moments. He made a conscious decision to pull together all that was teaching and to push aside all that was not. Frustration was getting the best of him. He had spent so much time beating his head against the wall, fighting battles that drained his spirit. *I keep getting drawn into the open to fight education's big fights. No more.* He had reconciled the fact that politics made hoop-jumping inevitable, but as long as he could close that door, he'd be fine.

His old friend and boss, Tom McIntyre had talked often about "ownership" of the classroom and as principal, had fought to preserve it. But the erosion of the classroom experience had started long before both of them even came along. Seat time for students was becoming more and more of a precious commodity, and those who fought for it came to be seen as outlaws, possessed by a neurotic obsession to control their environments. Most would plead guilty. It was a formidable task; with federal and state mandates; the relentless onslaught of standardized testing; and the invasive attitude of administrators and parents. Tom was gone now, along with so many others, and gone with them was the will to keep pristine the learning environment. The good principals — the ones who tried to shield the teachers from the onslaught — were retiring left and right. They were getting worn down by the politics. They were growing tired of fighting with angry teachers and battling with administrators who were drinking the kool-ade. Steadily, the new order crowded out the real; the authentic; the human. Less and less time could be spent interfacing with students…lecturing, discussing, conversing…

Through the years Quinn cultivated a roguish individualism that allowed him to survive. He did survive, even thrived, but there grew a distance between him and many of his colleagues, and it rubbed some the wrong way. Quinn could feel the space and tried to fill it with a circle of friends and a unique closeness to his students. But there was a cost for keeping people at arm's length. There was most certainly a cost.

There were days when he loved to walk down and sit with the lunch group, and just talk of small things and laugh. But most days he chose to sit there at his desk and catch his breath or find a place outside. Quinn never could explain the distance he put between himself and others…he just wasn't the easiest guy to get close to. Maybe it wasn't a space at all. Maybe he was just tired of talking. People liked to make more of something than was actually there. When he lectured, he taught hard, and he filled the room with energy and emotion. When he coached it was the same — get him going on a subject he loved and there was no shutting him up. But by the time he was done, Quinn was oftentimes emotionally and physically drained. He seemed happy sitting by himself.

Hopefully, this nice weather would carry over into the week and he could spend some time outdoors. Eating his lunch on the green bench in the commons area had become a favorite practice of solitude. Quinn didn't do it enough to call it a ritual. But when the humidity eased, he tried to get down there at least a few days a week.

Ironically, a man who spent his days talking never felt it necessary to simply fill up the air with chatter. Quinn learned to practice what he preached to his students, and would often just sit and listen. Like his good friend, JB, he was never afraid of the quiet. Quinn would find JB at Longdoggers, an airy establishment on the beach. The two would catch up on things and then sometimes sit with elbows on the bar and say nothing. JB was a bear of a man. He'd been hanging drywall in Melbourne for 35 years, and he seemed to know everyone in this town worth knowing. There were times when he reminded Quinn of an old Indian, rather than an old Irishman. When he did speak, though, he was worth listening to. Quinn would often hang on his words. There were times when he felt he'd learn more with his ass on a stool than with his nose in a book.

Things changed with the cough…the incessant hack which at times interrupted every sentence. It started a year ago Christmas. It became comical: *The Civil Rights (cough) Act of Nineteen Sixty (cough cough) Four outlawed (cough) dis(cough)crimina(cough)tion (cough cough cough!).* He had his bouts with bronchitis through the years, so he figured that's what it was, but then one morning while shaving he detected a small lump on his neck…what ended up being a swollen lymph node. Tests confirmed the doctor's suspicions: Lymphoma…Hodgkins Lymphoma Stage 2. Within a week he started chemotherapy. Spring soon turned into summer, and what a long strange summer it would be.

Although the prognosis was optimistic, and the treatment was tolerable, Quinn felt a sense of urgency to collect; to gather; to write. What was once a pursuit now became an obsession. Last summer, Quinn's reflections poured out of him. He began to read voraciously. Being confined to the house for much of the time, he felt driven to pull together something; everything; anything; and get it on paper. He cleaned up a collection of poems and then started work on these essays. He had no feeling of pending doom, mind you, and his writing wasn't driven by some perverted need to leave a mark. It seemed to be steered rather by a paternal instinct Quinn had toward teaching. He felt he needed to do something to protect it. He wanted to stand up and give his perspective.

Writing was liberating not merely because it provided him an outlet, but because it opened him up…his emotional and spiritual pores. Quinn's senses were now keener. He possessed a new awareness of everything around him. He was seeing things as Proust said, "with new eyes." To write meant to choose a particular way to live.

> "…the pure fact of living seemed like a new branch of theology."
> -Pat Conroy

However, when his health returned, his view changed on what he had written. Quinn spent the past month wrestling with his own arrogance. How could he be so presumptuous as to believe he had something to say — particularly about teaching? *When and how is it acceptable for me to write about teaching?* It was like speaking or writing about parenting or relationships, whereby the very act of expounding on such subjects was proof that you didn't know what the hell you were talking about!

Quinn remembered a certain priest whose homilies always held a firm grip upon him. It was because he was was so human. Father Karl never let himself become bigger than his message. He had an almost Lincoln-like ability to raise his lessons by lowering himself. And so it all comes back to humility. Remembering how losing his sense of self-importance was essential to becoming a decent teacher, Quinn now realized it was also vital to writing. He carried in his billfold a copy of something he'd written years ago while sitting alone by a fire on Ash Wednesday:

> *…and so it comes to this. I finally begin to try to lose my self-importance…finally understanding my sins of vanity and hypocrisy. My sense of purpose has been tainted by false humility. I have committed Eliot's treason in doing the right things for the wrong reasons, and it makes any feelings of achievement ring hollow. No more. Only now do I begin to realize what Jesus meant: we must make the journey down to become the very least. Maybe instead of being "known" as a good man, I try to become a good man. Perhaps*

now, instead of being known as a good teacher, it's time to actually become one. Maybe the drive to write will become pure...and come directly from the aching need for expression rather than the hollow need to be remembered...

Today

There is something good in today;
Something unique and particular about today.
In the face of fear and uncertainty;
Frustration and sadness;
Tedium and worry;
There is something that makes this a day like no other.
So, I keep my head up and my eyes open...

The Struggle

On Human Nature

> "Human history could not justify
> the Declaration of Independence
> and its large statements of the
> new idea; the nation went
> behind human history and
> appealed to human nature."
> -Theodore Parker[5]

Theodore Parker, a direct descendant of Concord hero Captain Robert Parker, was one of Abraham Lincoln's great influences. He had a firm grip on what we have here.

It's rather ironic, don't you think? Here I am writing on the importance of history to a people whose nation was founded upon a rejection of history. Here, people were freed from the old way of doing things. There was nothing linear about the establishment of America. The story of Europe is one of social, economic, political, and religious oppression. America jumped the tracks, so to speak; springing from a philosophical awakening that questioned every aspect of authority.

Our history is not Europe's history, and just as we rejected the history of the old world, we embraced a new legacy. The Enlightenment gave birth to the field of political science and Colonial America became a laboratory for its theories. People lived here for six generations relatively free of the yoke of aristocracy and tyranny. Their short history had proven what Enlightenment thinkers had claimed: the old way of doing things was not the only way. The Intellectual Revolution had found its validation.

Isaac Newton's attempts to scientifically explain nature would lead to attempts to scientifically explain society...and human

---

[5] Quoted in Garry Wills. *Lincoln at Gettysburg The Words that Remade America (New York: Simon and Schuster, 1992), 110.*

behavior. The belief in natural laws led to the belief in natural rights. Is it any wonder that John Locke, a man among the political thinkers of the age, is also considered the grandfather of behavioral psychology?

If America is the product of the debate over the hypothetical purpose of government, it is also then, the result of the philosophical argument over human nature. Thomas Hobbes laid the groundwork in *Leviathan*. He believed that any established form of government is rooted in the understanding of human nature. *Are we good or bad? Are we smart or stupid?* Although he believed we were born free, Hobbes had a very negative view of human nature, and he insisted that people need a strong military dictatorship to keep us in line. This claim of course became the baseline for the argument.

But the American Idea was bigger than those who embraced it. In defending the right of self-government, Jefferson himself wrote a check he couldn't cash. The principles of the Declaration of Independence ran head on into the peculiar institutions and values of early American life, but he got it planted, as Frost said, "and it will trouble us a thousand years."

Surely by establishing a nation upon the rejection of traditional forces of stability, we're asking for trouble. Over the past two centuries, any institution or condition that existed contrary to the principles of liberty and equality was eventually challenged. Those challenges, however, found new obstacles — new traditions; new old ways of doing things.

In Lincoln's time, the breach between our principles and practices was ever-widening. His attack on slavery was based solely on the Declaration of Independence. In elevating the Declaration from birth certificate to creed, Lincoln argued that the Founders were not saying that perfect equality and freedom actually existed. He believed they were throwing it out there as a goal; an ideal to be pursued.[6]

---

[6] Wills, *Lincoln at Gettysburg, 109, 110.*

By charging us with "finishing the work," and by calling on us to be so dedicated, Lincoln tapped into one of the fundamental aspects of Enlightenment thought: the individual's capacity for self-improvement. He tied it to the nation's capacity for improvement, and in so doing, moved us closer to our ideal.

Self-improvement requires self-criticism. It compels us to be painfully honest with ourselves. In the wake of both our failings and our accomplishments, the work continues: more justice; more freedom; less discrimination; more tolerance...

My father taught me that if you work for something; at something; toward something — if you work hard enough and long enough, the work becomes the something. So then, the foundation of American History is that struggle to bridge the gap between the real and the ideal. The struggle itself defines us.

NOTES:

- *In teaching the bad news, so to speak, we remind Americans of all the times we've fallen short of the ideal...*
- *It is important that we constantly return to the Idea...Jefferson and Lincoln in every chapter of American History*
- *Every story we tell of America must connect to the struggle (Sam Houston, John Kennedy, Bill Clinton...)*
- *I don't believe we can teach a survey course in American History without mentioning freedom, justice, and responsibility on a daily basis.*

October 14

Quinn sat himself down on the green bench in front of the school and pressed pause. He unwrapped a peanut-butter and honey sandwich and took a bite. It was orange blossom honey he bought from the Harvey's Groves store on 192. Two ladies in there had sworn that it would help with his cough. It didn't do the trick, but it sure tasted good.

Either way it was a beautiful day and he had come outside to enjoy it. *"Blue skies and Ultraviolet rays,"* he sang to himself, invoking an old Jimmy Buffett line for the occasion. He had made a habit of dropping whatever he was doing when he heard the outdoors calling. It was so easy to get wrapped up in the tasks at hand that the wonders of the day could slip on by. Quinn was determined not to let that happen. Brian Williams had revealed the awful news the night before: Florida was now the third largest state in the union. Quinn groaned at the thought. His grandfather had foretold Florida's fate long ago. *"Air conditioning and Disney – they will be our undoing. Mark my words."*

Quinn did mark them and thought of all the spineless greedy politicians who contributed to the fall. Still, on days like this it was hard to blame anyone for wanting to be down here. Seventy five degrees, slight breeze out of the north, and a clear sky so blue it defied description. As hard as they tried, they couldn't completely destroy paradise. Not yet, at least. Today was nothing short of glorious…a fine October afternoon, and Quinn decided to enjoy it.

"Mind if I sit?" A young woman with dark hair and sunglasses sat down beside him.

"No, not at all," Quinn lied. "Not at all."

"I see you sitting out here," she said. "My classroom is right up there," pointing in the general direction of the stairs.

"I'm Frank Quinn. I can't believe we haven't met."

"That sounded almost creepy, but I'm okay with it. I'm Jodi Richardson."

Quinn was oblivious as usual. He repeated her name to himself. He had the terrible habit of forgetting a person's name right after the introduction.

"Well, how are you?" Quinn asked cordially.

"Fine, how are you?" she said.

"What do you teach, Jodi?"

"English," she said. "Frank Quinn. That sounds like an old name."

"I'm an old guy," Quinn replied. "It's an Irish name—Francis Tiernan Quinn. I share it with a grandfather I never met and a grandson I never knew."

There was a long silence. "I'm not sure I have anything to say after that."

She made eye contact for a moment and then started to laugh, breaking the tension. "How come you sit outside by yourself," she asked, returning to her line of questioning.

"I like being by myself, and besides, I guess I've driven everybody off."

"Not everybody...yet," she said.

Quinn wasn't quite sure he wanted this exchange to go any further. He coveted his time alone on the bench and this woman was taking him in directions he did not care to go.

"I've heard some things about you," she said curiously.

"What have you heard of me, Ms. …Richardson, is it?

"I heard you're a dinosaur; and yes it's Richardson. And I heard you love it."

"Love what?" asked Quinn.

"Teaching…kids…you teach history, right?"

"American History, among other things," Quinn replied.

"Other things? And after all these years you still love it? How's that possible?" she said.

"You know," Quinn paused. "No one's ever asked me that."

"I'm asking."

"You're awfully curious about an old burnout sitting on a bench." *And bold,* he thought. Quinn glanced down at his watch; Jodi took the cue and got up to leave.

"It was nice finally meeting you, Francis Tiernan Quinn."

"It was nice meeting you, Jodi."

"Maybe, I'll see you down here again," she said

"I'll be here...hopefully, every chance I get," said Quinn.

A voice came from behind him "Who was that?"

"I don't know, someone feeling sorry for me."

Ray plopped down beside him. "What in the hell are you doing out here? Shouldn't you be wearing sunscreen or something?"

"Just sittin here noticing things, Ray. I read once that Mark Twain was a great noticer."

"Yeah, well I noticed you didn't make the faculty meeting this morning, Mr. Quinn."

Frank was oblivious. "I like to come out here every once in a while."

"Oh, I see, you won't come by the lunch crowd, but you'll sit out here by yourself."

"It's funny," Quinn mused, "how if one person slows down from the hurried pace, it reminds others to do the same. Normally, folks pass each other briskly; if you're lucky, you'll get a polite hello, maybe a nod of the head or smile. But when I sit here on this bench all sorts of people stop to talk. Even when I don't want 'em to!"

"Well, thank you for taking it upon yourself to slow down the whole human race. I can smell the roses as we speak!" They both laughed and Quinn raised the middle finger.

"You know, Frank, this is your weirdo side."

"Better than my drunk side."

"Got me there." Ray shook his head.

"Ever notice how teachers can't talk about education without discussion becoming a *bitchfest?*" Quinn asked out of the blue.

"There you go noticing again," Ray said. "What's a *bitchfest* and where in the hell did this come from?"

"Seriously," Quinn went on. "We can't talk about things without it turning into a forum on how hard and undervalued our jobs are."

Ray folded his arms.

"I read something online last night," Quinn continued. "It started out pretty good…a couple exchanges of insight, then boom, the complaints started raining down. I don't have enough time on the planet for that shit."

"It's what we do best," Ray assured him. "Complain and then go back to work. How are the grandbabies?"

Quinn rolled on without acknowledging Ray's attempt to change the subject. "Well, it pisses me off. And I bet it annoys the hell out of people outside the profession, too. It makes them stop listening."

"Well, what should we do then?" It wasn't that Ray wasn't a hardass. He just didn't seem like he was in the mood to hear the rant. But Quinn on the other hand was certainly in the mood to rant or vent or whatever this was.

"Start complaining about the right things! Stop bitching about bad pay. You knew that going in. Stop expecting gratitude. Do the right thing for the right reason. Love your country! Close your eyes every night and know you tried to help your country."

"Did you script this?"   Ray checked his phone and got up to leave. He didn't wear a watch.

"Well, that was a quick visit, Mr. Donohue." Quinn tripped the switch and was immediately out of rant mode.

"You have a way of making people want to get up and go," Ray said. "Besides, the bell's about to ring, genius," and he started to walk away.

Quinn was oddly amused. "Yeah, folks tend to like me...but they never like me for long!"

 Then he finished the rest of his sandwich.

Communities of Memory

… Social Cohesion begins with History

Some say history is dead.
Hush now, children, don't you fret!
Robert Nesta Marley said
We can't forget
For the sake of some bright future!
Island songs give spirits lift
And yet, we wonder why we drift.
The rhythm moves us on this day
But rhyme and reason seem so far away.

It's safe to say that many people are bored with history because they see no relevance…no connection. The paradox lies in the possibility that a person's aversion to learning history may well be caused by his or her feelings of alienation, but the discovery of a common past is the first step in *reconnecting* with other members of society.

Regardless of whether we are speaking of an ethnic community, a religious community, or even a national community, the group is constituted by its past. Bonds of friendship are measured by sayings such things as, "we go way back." Relationships and careers are marked by anniversaries and landmarks. With apologies to my priest, when I fall to my knees, I am praying as my father did; and my father's father; and his father.

In *Habits of the Heart,* Robert Bellah described this sense of connectedness as *"a community of memory."* Right here we find another valuable reason to learn history. Whether we are talking of your family or your nation, in learning your story, you can discover the marrow of community--its hopes, fears, and values are found in the lives of its people. In retelling its story, a group "offers examples of the men and the women who have exemplified the meaning of community."[7] Such stories contain conceptions of character and the

---

[7] Bellah, 153.

definitive virtues that make up that character. As I said before, we learn of men and women who have lived responsible and joyful lives.

A society rooted in the protection and expansion of individual freedom and dignity has also produced an epidemic of alienation, cynicism, and apathy among its members. Many lament the lack of community. They believe it's impossible for people to see themselves sharing a common life. Modern America is described as a random collection of individuals; lacking harmony, solidarity, and fraternity.

What is this community and why is it important? What does the individual owe his community, anyway? When do individual rights give way to the rights of the community? Or should they ever? Community implies solidarity…union. People are bound together by a consensus over what is right, good, and useful. It's a conscious state of interdependence that transcends rather than obscures self-interest.

The ties that bind can be cultural, regional, religious, or even national. Almost always, feelings of community are temporary, but even through these intermittent rushes, community can serve as a middle ground where private and public interests can be reconciled without the interference of government.

> *There are three hundred million of us!*
> *I've got my music--you've got yours*
> *And they tell me we are tied*
> *By some belief that only living free can bring?*

Individuals have been splintered largely because of a social and political environment that encourages it. Nineteenth century observer Alexis de Tocqueville first identified Americans' tendency to isolate ourselves and **"withdraw into a circle of family and friends…leaving the greater society to look after itself."**[8] The end result of this isolation is the citizen becoming an island; forgetting his ties to his ancestors, his contemporaries, and even his descendants.

To be sure, this tendency is not the Emersonian individualism that is so essential to self-determination, nor is it just the selfish

---

[8] Alexis de Tocqueville. *Democracy in America*, George Lawrence translation, ed. JP Mayer (New York: Harper and Row, 1969), 508.

egoism frequently thrown about these days. It's what Tocqueville called "a calm considered feeling" leading people to soothe their sense of insignificance by drawing into a closed circle.[9]

This turning inward is compensation. Mass democracy makes men and women feel weak and unimportant in public life. As society grows larger and more diverse, we tend to feel smaller. The more insignificant we feel in public life, the more we retreat into private circles. The further inward we turn, the less relevant we see public life. Oftentimes, my students have grown up in households that have completely withdrawn. Their upbringings have been completely apolitical, and it's a major obstacle in reaching them.

> "Each man is forever thrown back
> on himself alone, and there is danger
> that he may be shut up in the solitude
> of his own heart."
> – Tocqueville[10]

Tocqueville saw this isolation as quite dangerous to freedom because of the vulnerability it creates. By devoting himself to private life, the citizen estranges himself from politics, and thereby loses a vital protection against each and every form of tyranny. The mess in Washington today may cause many more to withdraw, but perhaps we should recognize the possibility that government gridlock is the product of "leaving society to look after itself.

There are many reasons for this inward turning of citizens, and also many remedies. Where do we start? The tension between community and the individual lies at the core of the American Idea. In *Habits of the Heart*, Bellah claimed that the roots of social cohesion can be found in the past. Surely there are other forces at work here, and trying to pin down everything that unites or divides us is a daunting task, but Bellah insisted that it begins with history.[11]

---

[9] Ibid.
[10] Ibid.
[11] Bellah, 153.

Living a courageous, virtuous life doesn't guarantee an easy go of it. It will not assure happiness, or even stature and popularity. It doesn't even promise a positive place in the hearts and minds of posterity. The story of Robert E. Lee is proof positive. Lee is among the most virtuous people I have ever read about, yet his place in American History is in a dark corner.

When I speak of Lee to my students, I remind them of the terrible ironies life can offer. In our struggles to live responsible and purposeful lives, there is many a slippery slope; but none more perilous than righteousness. We must be true to ourselves in our motives. If I think that leading a virtuous life will bring fame and fortune, I am sadly mistaken. Lee's decision to go against the Union and with Virginia was gut-wrenching to say the least. He delayed sending his letter of resignation from the U.S. Army for a day because he said it was so painful. Although Lee's defense of his decision was that he could not raise his hand against home and family, many of his friends and family members sided with the Union. He was stuck with an impossible decision.

So here is a great, honorable man whose fate dealt him a tough hand. Lee was a man of great dignity, but he died bitter, angry, and disappointed. The "Eliot-trap" we may fall into–by doing the right thing for the wrong reason – is deep and dark. Doing good has its own rewards. And sometimes, its own punishment.

That said, it's important to teach the bad news. History must also tell of the pain and tragedy; of the suffering both received and inflicted. Just as families pass down stories of the trials and tribulations of parents and grandparents, a nation must chronicle its history, and it is this meaning of community that can serve as a cohesive force in the fragmented society that is America. We participate in rituals, ethics, and aesthetics which define our way of life. Bellah called them "practices of commitment," for within them there are "patterns of loyalty and obligation that connect us."

October 17

"Did I ever tell you the first time I saw Frank Quinn?" Ray bellowed.

He loved to tell this story. Four or five younger teachers were gathered at Meg's for an impromptu celebration of Quinn's birthday. Ray had already put down a few Budweisers and he'd kicked into story-teller mode.

"It was in the old gym…district playoff game…coldest damn basketball game ever!" Melbourne High School's gymnasium was a relic. No heat. No air conditioning. Half of the windows were busted out. It wasn't rare to see a pigeon fly through. There were notorious dead spots in the gym floor which gave a distinct advantage to the home team, when trapping the opponent.

"It was so cold," Ray said with a laugh in his voice, "that you could see the players' breath as they ran up and down the court."

It was indeed a freezing February evening. The gym was packed with bundled up fans. They resembled a crowd more prepared to watch a football game in Pittsburgh than a basketball game in Florida.

"Standing in the far corner near the exit, by the home bench was this big bear of a guy—long shaggy hair, beard, flannel shirt and flip-flops. The best part," Ray explained, "was this bright red Hawaiian shirt hanging out from under the flannel."

"Style knows itself," Quinn said, after the laughter stopped.

"Style?" Ray said sarcastically. "I was sure a homeless guy had slipped into the gym!"

"Well it sure wasn't to get warm," Quinn said, smiling and sipping on a beer. "I'll say that much."

"What were you doing?" somebody asked.

"I was covering the game for the Melbourne Times."

"The Melbourne Times?" said someone else. "Never heard of it."

"Too young," Quinn said with the leverage of an old man talking to a younger one.

"Nick Wright had some good teams back then," Ray remembered.

"Nick Wright? Was that the guy who looked like Mark Twain?"

Quinn laughed. "Good coach, good teacher, good writer. Yeah, he became a good friend. I heard he went back to Arkansas. Spending his retirement writing books on the Civil War.

"So, any plans for the big day?" Ray patted him on the back. Quinn shrugged and smiled. "Where you watching the Gators? Ray asked.

"Probably with Jim," Quinn answered. "Giants-Cardinals tomorrow night." October was their favorite month — college football and the MLB postseason. Ray listed the games that weekend.

"Yeah buddy," Quinn agreed. "Probably won't get out of the recliner,"

"Well come on by if you feel like it," Ray offered, but he knew Quinn would probably pass. Both were hard core Florida Gators, and they were deeply superstitious. Decades of living and dying with the Orange and Blue had led both of them to believe that there was some sort of jinx when they watched together.

Quinn drove home and was greeted by the dogs like it was, as always, Christmas morning. He warmed up a cup of coffee in the microwave and went out to the porch. He thought back on a verse he'd written long ago:

> *I got up early Thursday and slipped out quietly*
> *So not to wake my wife and son and daughter.*
> *I drove across the causeway to celebrate my birthday*
> *Watching the sun rise out of the water.*
> *It had spent the last three months boiling the Atlantic:*
> *A hurricane was brewing five hundred miles from here.*
> *Still I observed my pagan ritual for the passing of a year:*
> *With a thermos and a cooler — hot coffee and cold beer.*

He thought maybe that he and the dogs should renew the ritual tomorrow morning.

To the Ticking Clock

Where he once could not abide
To chronicle the time or tide,
He's taken now to wear a watch
On quiet walks downtown.
Is it innocence revisited?
Wisdom lost or found?
He's given now to sip his scotch
Where once he gulped it down.

And to keep his mind unbound —
To see the beauty all around;
He now lifts his head up from the grind.
Paying close attention,
When once he paid no mind.

Now he flies away on daydreams,
Not shackled to the ground.
Where once he spread his life so thin,
Now, he boils it down.

Something Good

...happiness is not always a state of unbridled joy. It can be a feeling of calm contentment in finding something good about this day; and the warm expectancy of finding something good in tomorrow.

October 24

"So, how'd you like it?"

"You know me. Of course some of that shit—I had no idea what you were talking about."

Ray pushed the manila folder over to Quinn. "Frank, why are you writing this?"

"What do you mean, why am I writing this?" Quinn looked forlorn.

"Why are you doing this?" Ray seemed almost protective of Quinn, maybe fearing that his reckless idealism would make him a fool. Ray's sensitivities for his profession often appeared calloused over. But Quinn knew down deep, that he still had some passion. "We have another boss to break in and here you are pontificating…"

Quinn didn't answer. He took a drink of beer, held it in his mouth for a moment, then swallowed.

"You know me, Frank…"

"Just say it, Ray,"

Ray always did have license to say anything to Quinn so he pushed it. "You're taking yourself a bit seriously, aren't you?"

"Yeah, I am."

"Some of this sounds like it's coming from some guy handing out pamphlets downtown."

"I told you before, Ray, I am worn down by the stuff we have to hear every day. Whatever we do is not good enough for the talking heads. I'm tired of the friggin' orthodoxy.

"I love teaching, Ray, and I figured out last summer that I love it for a whole bunch of reasons and it's time someone talked about that part! We were good teachers, Ray, both of us. And when they leave us alone, we're still good! I can't tell you how many times I'd come in to get coffee through Chris' room and just sit in there listening to you tell stories. "

"But they won't leave us alone, Frank," Ray sighed. "And do you think this is gonna change anything?"

"Probably not. But I just can't go along to get along." Quinn leaned back and crossed his arms. "All these reforms, they're saying the same thing…that we don't know what the hell we're doing."

"When did you ever go along?" Ray had the look of someone who wished he was somewhere else. "Aren't you the guy who skipped faculty meetings for a year and a half?"

"They never missed me," Quinn answered, and that was true.

"Let's see, didn't you rip the phone line out of the wall? And break the intercom with a baseball bat?"

"That was a long time ago, I've mellowed. What are you getting at?" asked Quinn. He could feel himself getting irritated.

"And they stopped inviting you to Baccalaureate after you managed to insult every major religion! Tell me, Quinn, how do you piss off the Methodists?"

Quinn had to laugh. "Yeah, they weren't too thrilled with the story about Jefferson cutting up the Bible. Ray, why are you bringing all this up?"

"Because that was the Quinn I liked…and the one everybody else liked too. The table-thumping, rule-breaking son of a bitch who acted like he didn't care if he got fired from one day to the next! Who was going to have it his way no matter what."

"We were both flying by the seat of our pants," Quinn reminded him.

"So what changed?" Ray asked. "When did you become this Old Testament prophet leading teachers out of the frigging wilderness? I worry."

"You worry?"

"I worry that you're burning bridges you didn't even know were there."

"It's a little late in the game to be thinking about that," Quinn said. "Maybe I remember the way things were…maybe I don't mind going down in flames. And it's pretty ironic that you should talk of burning bridges!"

"That's not my point, Frank." Ray picked up the folder. "Half the stuff in here, you need a doctorate to understand."

"Because we don't teach it," Quinn answered, too loud for the room, holding his hands in the air. "It becomes strange and unfamiliar."

"You're becoming strange and unfamiliar!" Ray shot back. "Why do you spend so much fucking time on that freedom and individualism stuff? I mean…you keep saying it over and over again."

"Because freedom is more than just being left alone," Quinn answered. "That's the roots, Ray," Quinn said. "As Willie Dixon would say, *the rest is the fruits.*" Quinn seemed happy with his reply.

Ray stared straight ahead, scraping at the label of his Budweiser bottle. He gritted his teeth and shook his head. Finally, after the long pause, he said, "Is it possible for you to put one fucking sentence together without quoting someone? Usually someone I've never fucking heard of!

"You never heard of Willie Dixon?"

"Oh, fuck you, Frank!"

"Fuck me? Fuck you!" There was a long silence. "Ah…you're right Ray," Quinn said. "Fuck me…swingin."

They didn't cuss each other very often, but when they did, there was one recurring figure of speech. But the wheels were turning now and Ray Donohue was about to get his money's worth.

"You want an answer? Here's your friggin' answer," said Quinn, and then he cut loose. "I think America is more than a geographic expression…more than a goddamned military and economic superpower. If we get away from who we are, if we lose our identity, then we're no more, no better than any of those other friggin civilizations who have come and gone! We have to remember, Ray…but nope, we live in the United States of Amnesia and we're sliding down a dark hole. And our great grandchildren will be no fucking better off than our great grandparents when they were stuck back in Ireland. Ha! At least the Irish remember their own misery!"

Quinn hadn't realized how loud he'd gotten. Lots of eyes were on him.

"Everything okay, guys?" Karen the bartender asked.

"We're fine," Ray assured her. "Just trying to save the country."

Quinn finished his Guinness and looked around. "I have no idea why I'm writing this, Ray. All I know is that I need to."

Ray patted him on the back. "That's good enough for me." But for the first time in a long while, Frank Quinn was the first to leave the bar.

The First Form of Understanding...

The Role of Art and Literature in Teaching American History

I do love books. Especially old ones. I love the smell of them. I like the feel of the worn pages. There is a humanness to them. I once bought a Hemingway biography off of a shelf in a restaurant. It was placed there as a decoration, for crying out loud. I don't recall much about the dinner, but the rescued book is still there upon my shelf, waiting for yet another visit.

I like to think of all the times a book was opened. Who was the reader? Was she sitting in a rocker or a recliner? In front of a fire or out on the porch? Was he sipping good whiskey or hot coffee? Was there a dog at his feet? Did she have music playing? And so it is with the stories and ideas that spring from the books.

Hemingway himself said that after reading a good book, it all belongs to you. Books, poems, and paintings can draw you in. Before I can even attempt to make history come alive for my students, it must first come alive for me. And for that to happen, it must be human. It must be filled with stories of men and women doing great and good things; of complicated people and simple truths.

I once heard an account of how Jefferson wrote the Declaration of Independence while holed up in a modest room in Philadelphia. It struck me that aside from pen and paper, and wine and cheese, all he had was his violin. He'd write awhile and play the fiddle awhile; write some more, then play some more. I guess it's not a stretch to say our nation was played into existence. Jefferson himself instinctively knew the power of music.

You know, I'm not quite sure if I could give a lesson on Thomas Jefferson without telling that particular story. I can't imagine teaching the text of the Declaration without also teaching the context of its creation. While in Philadelphia, Jefferson lost two daughters, a son, and his mother. Back in Virginia, his wife was too grief-stricken to get out of bed. Still under those circumstances, he wrote what Lincoln would later call, *"the immortal emblem of humanity."* Damn...

The American Declaration of Independence stands on its own. It's up to us the living to realize what we have here. Nevertheless, the human drama behind its creation strengthens its grip on me. I am struck by the motives and politics of the members of Congress; the huge sacrifices, struggles, and tragedies in their lives; the irony of establishing ideals and principles that few could live up to. These things make it all the more amazing. Stories of the relationships between Adams and Jefferson, and the power of George Washington's leadership, bolster our understanding of human nature. Understanding human nature; isn't that what America is all about? According to Robert Frost, poetry is *the first form of understanding* each other, and ourselves.[12]

The more comfortable I am with the subject, the more creative I can be with the lesson. True, we must rein in the student's curiosity so he or she can focus on the task at hand, but narrative history is about discovering the plot. If a teacher knows his song well, he can give his students more latitude for discovery.

But there's more...much more. The lecture needs rhythm. It needs irony and pathos. And it needs place. All of these things can be taken from poetry.

In our noble efforts to tell the stories of great change in the world — wars and depression; revolution and oppression; liberation and occupation; mass migrations and convulsions within or without — we often smother the lives of the individuals. History loses its humanity. It takes on the appearance of an irresistible natural force, resembling an earthquake or tornado. Poetry reminds us of our humanity. It puts faces back on the characters and breathes the human spirit back into their bodies. Those we've lost in wars weren't just statistics. They were sons and fathers and husbands...uncles and cousins.

---

[12] Quoted in Harvey Breit, *The Writer Observed* (1956, as cited in *Poetry Foundation*.) Retrieved from http://www.poetryfoundation.org/bio/robert-frost

"... on the banks, unnoticed, people build homes,
make love, raise children, sing songs, write poetry,
and even whittle statues."
-Will Durant

This is not to say that we should gloss over any of the monumental events of American History. On the contrary, let's spend more time on them. But by weaving the personal dramas into the stories, we can preserve the gravity of those events. They don't get lost on a timeline.

The only risk of using art and literature in lessons on war and depression is the fact that students aren't used to it. Public education has taught them to compartmentalize. They may well indulge their English teacher for forty seven minutes, "but what is Langston Hughes doing in my History class?" Before we can convince students to cross over, we must be brave enough, or reckless enough to jump in ourselves.

Historian Shelby Foote was a self-described novelist who spent decades writing history, and I too find myself a writer, in the sense that I believe history is best presented as a narrative; a story; a spoken or written account of connected events. When I heard Foote read an excerpt from his own text, I realized why he called himself a narrative historian.

Foote's understanding of writing history shaped my understanding of teaching it. He based his approach on a paradox proclaimed by Oscar Wilde that nature imitates art instead of the other way around. I can't help but agree. As Foote said, "Once the painter saw colors in shadows, shadows took on colors for the first time."[13]

I've loved the ocean all of my life, but Hemingway made me see the countless shades of green and blue. I never fully appreciated the taste of oysters until after I read his description of eating them. Pat Conroy once spent a page and a half describing a moonrise, and after

---

[13] Quoted in "Interviews," *Shelby Foote, The Art of Fiction No. 158 (The Paris Review, Summer 1999).* Retrieved from http://www.theparisreview.org/interviews/931/the-art-of-fiction-no-158-shelby-foote

reading that, I don't think I've ever been the same. Art and literature help us see the world, and at times, can lead a passive student to places he never dreamed he'd care to go.

Foote believed his task to be one of discovering a plot in a part of history just as that painter found colors in shadows. He insisted that anything he could learn about putting words together helped him write history. That said, anything I can learn about the words can help me teach history.

To be true to our Creed, we must tell the story of America through the eyes of individuals struggling in their pursuit of meaning, purpose, and fulfillment. The story of government and leaders should be in the context of either aiding or obstructing the individual's search. When my students were assigned the task of asking grandparents what they considered to be the most important events of American History, more of them mentioned the War for Independence than the Declaration of Independence itself. It was apparent that at least for that generation, a creed was only as strong as our will to fight for it. In again borrowing from Kennedy, American History must speak to our deepest strengths — "not to our size but to our spirit; not to our political beliefs but to our insight; not to our self-esteem but to our self-comprehension."[14]

In believing that poetry was that first form of understanding, Frost was always looking to the natural world for metaphors of the human condition. His characters were often retreating to the woods to save their self-direction and resistance, swearing off the modern world and all its trappings:

> "It is this backward motion toward the source
> Against the stream, that most we see ourselves in..."
> -from West-Running Brook

Thoreau had gone to the woods to find his identity, but to Frost, the New Hampshire woods served as a refuge...a place to protect him from the forces that strip a human of all authenticity.

---

[14] *President John F. Kennedy: Remarks at Amherst College, October 26, 1963.* Retrieved from http://arts.gov/about/kennedy.

Where does that fit in the scheme of American History? Well, if in fact Jefferson is right, and the very essence of America rests upon the right of the individual to search for his own meaning, how then can art and literature not be a vehicle of that search? Frost steered clear of politics and religion, but he offers through his characters' conflicts a practical way to understand the individual's struggle with the American Idea.

Although Jefferson was certainly a creature of the New World, a product of "the new beginning," free from the old ways, he loved the culture of Europe. He loved the music, philosophy, poetry, and art. But Jefferson saw it as unable to improve the human condition. Europe in his eyes was "a land of eternal war and tyranny." Maybe European art served too much as an escape; as a place to run to avoid whatever monster was coming down the street this time; to flee the ravages of hatred and greed.[15] There remains that vivid image of a young priest sitting in his basement playing the cello waiting for the Gestapo. He would survive to become Pope John Paul II.

In contrast, American art and literature doesn't serve as an escape, but as a force that moves us toward self-understanding. Perhaps American art is not as great as European art, but there is an edgy authenticity to it that makes it ours. Through our art, we can see ourselves. In Thoreau or Whitman; Emily Dickinson or Billie Holiday; Bob Dylan or Louis Armstrong; we discover the fabric of democracy.

Poetry and Place

Creating a sense of belonging to a part of the natural world is yet another force that makes history palpable in our lives. On other pages, I've talked about how sharing memories connects us and helps us establish a sense of place. Through art we learn that place can also be a powerful means of drawing students into a story. Not only is place an essential component of context, which helps us understand and appreciate the circumstances and setting of an event, it can also bring an event or character to life.

---

[15] Jacob Needleman, *The American Soul, Rediscovering the Wisdom of the Founders* (New York: Penguin Putnam Inc., 2002), 287.

Geography is so much more than memorizing states and rivers. It's not less, by the way. It's important to know where Kentucky is. But it's also good to know how the wind blows across the Great Plains; how hot the summers are in Philadelphia; how cold it gets in Michigan; and what the Rockies look like.

The sense of connection to place is rooted in stories, maps, pictures, and art. Over time, experiences strengthen a person's bond to place. Unfortunately, we teachers rarely have the time or resources to transport our students to actual historic sites. But if we can follow the lead of the poet and pull the listener into the story by letting her shiver or sweat with the characters, we may have something. If I can figuratively transport the student to a place, he may have greater empathy for those involved.

Oftentimes, students have visited historic sites on family vacations. They are eager to share stories of their travels to battlefields, monuments, national parks, and other landmarks. They quickly become witnesses to the power of place. No lecture can quite capture Gettysburg; or the Grand Canyon; or Monticello. Still, words, as Lincoln said, are "as necessary as they are inadequate." I encourage all of my students to visit the places we study, some time in their lives. Leaving class should be the beginning and not the end of their American History lessons.

Poetry and Voice

No matter how fired up I am about my lesson; regardless of how solid my background is on the subject at hand; it needs an effective delivery. Even for the most engaged student, the nature of the presentation will have a huge impact on comprehension and retention. In crafting one's delivery, this is where gut feelings kick in. It's instinctive. I would be dishonest if I said otherwise. History can be tedious, monotonous, and dry. Without "a voice," even the most curious student can be lost.

In poetry, we learn the importance of voice. By voice, I mean more than tone, volume, and intensity. I'm talking about the natural rhythms of speech. We can never forget that we're talking to students, not at them. Natural spoken speech is much different than the diction of professors, journalists, and textbook authors. Oftentimes, we abandon our natural voice in an effort to sound professorial. We want our audience to believe we know what the hell we're talking about, so we trade the vernacular for an artificial speech that lacks both rhythm and realism.

Think of the voices you love to hear: Morgan Freeman; Robert Duvall; Maya Angelou; James Earl Jones; Johnny Cash. I believe Maya Angelou could have read the ingredients on a cereal box, and I would have been captivated. In each of these voices, we hear the rhythm of poetry.

Poetry teaches us the significance of sentence sounds. We discover the difference between the right word and the almost-right word, and we learn to necklace those words together. Perhaps the true genius of Robert Frost is found in his ability to capture the lyrical essence of natural spoken speech.[16] Whether it be the dialect or the pace, Frost used the voice of the people to somehow make his words both lyrical and realistic. It took me a long time to figure that out, too.

Now, just because you don't have Morgan Freeman's voice quality doesn't mean you can't capture your audience. I've been speaking with a dull monotone for decades. My sinuses have been closed since the Reagan Administration. That doesn't mean your voice can't work. Years ago, I found a vinyl recording of Frost reciting his poetry and it knocked me for a loop. A boy from the South had never heard such a tone or dialect. However, after listening to his readings over and over, his poems took on new meaning, as I was now able to hear his voice each time I picked up his collected works. Critics have faulted Frost for trying to create his style from the style of conversation, but that may well be one of his biggest contributions.

In my freshman year of college, I came across a History professor by the name of Frank Merritt. Each Sunday, Professor Merritt played the organ in the Baptist Church, but during the week,

---

[16] *The Literary Essays of Ezra Pound* (New York: New Directions, 1954), (as cited in *Poetry Foundation*.) Retrieved from http://www.poetryfoundation.org/bio/robert-frost

his religion was American History. He started lecturing ten minutes early and finished five minutes late. Speaking with a thick Tennessee accent, he was a story-teller; an actor. I can still hear that voice bouncing off the back wall, as he dragged us through every battle of the Civil War; each New Deal program; and every clause in the Constitution. His class was a splendid grind. There was rhythm. There was emotion. There was poetry.

Before I even got to college, I had been blessed with good teachers. Perhaps the best teacher I ever encountered was my 11th grade Social Studies teacher, Cathy Ford. She would have been great in any era.

We learned to be meticulous note-takers; good researchers; effective public speakers; and responsible citizens. And we learned to ask questions and find answers...all in one semester.

There was an exuberance in her lectures and discussions that I have never witnessed before or since. Without a doubt, it was among the most intellectually challenging courses I have taken at any level, but I remember laughing more in that class than any other. Mrs. Ford's good humor permeated the room. There was an infectious joy; and intoxication with knowledge that changed me forever.

She was an accomplished student in her own right, also holding an advanced degree in English. Perhaps many of her literary allusions raced right by me, but I was still in awe of her depth of knowledge. I recall working up the courage to ask her to read some things I had written. Mrs. Ford graciously agreed. My teacher's response is one I've carried all the while: "Before you write, learn the classics."

It was then that I began to devour the works of Frost, Twain, Hemingway, and even a little Shakespeare. It was here that I discovered the natural rhythms that blur the lines between poetry and prose.

Understanding the importance of rhythms and being able to employ them are two different things. Good lectures don't require the abandonment of grammar and syntax, but oftentimes, a rough edge —

a coarseness — can aid in the speech becoming both lyrical and authentic.

The artist teaches us that the voice of the messenger can breathe life into the message. Furthermore, by creating vivid images of the characters, the weather, the scenery, and even the food, he can take us to another place in time. Technology, in all its glory, has yet to catch up with the power of art and literature.

Lincoln and his Words

"In the short and simple annals of the
poor, it seems there are people
who breathe with the earth
and take into their lungs and blood some
of the hard and dark strength of its mystery."
-Carl Sandburg[17]

November 19, 1863. It seems like every road in the
man's life led to that day. He spoke for two and a half minutes. In
giving a "few appropriate remarks" at Gettysburg, few realized the
gravity of those three paragraphs. In time however, we will come to
understand that Abraham Lincoln will define us as a culture — what
we were, what we are, and what we may become. At the time,
Thomas Jefferson's Declaration of Independence was revered as our
founding document — our national birth certificate. But his
proposition of freedom and equality was so radical, it seemed beyond
our ken. Surely, they were lofty, noble ideas, but they seemed to hold
little relevance to everyday life in America. It will be Lincoln who
connects people to their values. Is there no greater challenge for a
leader? Is there no greater calling for a writer?

Is it possible for a political leader to be a philosopher? Can the
man who led a republic in war be its best hope for peace? The
American Idea reveals itself in many different forms. America
depends heavily upon arts and literature, for the artist is tied to this
great experiment with democracy. Art establishes what John
Kennedy called "the basic human truths which must serve as the
touchstones of our judgment." In his eulogy of Frost, Kennedy
claimed that art plays a vital role in a democracy, not as propaganda,
but truth, and it serves as a last check on power:

---

[17] Carl Sandburg, *Abraham Lincoln, The Prairie Years 2,* (New York: Harcourt Brace
and Company, 1926), *356.*

"When power leads man toward arrogance, poetry reminds him
of his limitations. When power narrows areas of man's concern, poetry
reminds him of the richness and diversity of his existence. When power
corrupts, cleanses."
–John F. Kennedy[18]

But what I was going to say when truth broke in with all her
matter of fact about art and democracy, is that volumes have been
written analyzing Lincoln's actions and motives, but only recently
have we begun to realize the power and resonance of his words.
Leadership is more than management, decision-making, and skillful
persuasion. It is the expression of vision. Words can do more than
inspire, or define great sacrifices. They can identify the values which
make life worth living; worth defending; worth dying for. Words can
challenge us to move ever closer to things we believe in. In his
speeches and writings, Lincoln presents a dialectic by which people
can take a great leap toward their ideals. He may well be one of the
most important writers in the history of Western civilization.

At the root of his rhetoric was an abiding faith in the people.
Nevertheless, he was haunted by the hypocrisy of his nation. How
could a country profess to love liberty while denying it to millions?
Lincoln spent little time and energy condemning Americans for living
such a lie. On the contrary, he believed that by appealing to "the
better angels of our nature," free men would see the error of their
ways.

Lincoln's argument began with elevating the ideals of the
Declaration of Independence. In contrast to Jefferson, who had no real
metaphysical attachment to the ideals he expressed, Lincoln was a
product of the Transcendentalist period. As a romantic, he hailed the
Declaration as a pledge "to all people of all colors everywhere"[19] His
premise is a lofty one—a person's reverence for freedom and equality
would lead him away from institutions that contradict such values.
So, the first step in ending the hypocrisy of slavery is *reminding* free
men of their ideals. Although this would be his recurring theme for
decades, Lincoln's consummate message is the Gettysburg Address.
With 272 words, he takes the American Idea and makes it the
American Creed:

---

[18] Kennedy, *Remarks at Amherst.*
[19] Quoted in Wills, *Lincoln at Gettysburg,* 105.

> "... a new nation, conceived in liberty and dedicated
> to the proposition that all men are created equal..."

The conflict with the Creed, of course, is the great struggle over slavery and the definition of freedom. I recall reading that Lincoln insisted on calling the institution "American slavery," rather than "African slavery," to emphasize the burden of our national dilemma. Throughout his political life, some of his most powerful words were built upon the contradiction of principle and practice:

> "Those who enjoy freedom and deny it to others
> deserve it not for themselves, and under a just God,
> cannot long retain it"

> "A house divided against itself cannot stand..."

On the surface, the "house divided" quote appears to be addressing the divisions between North and South, but Lincoln was also alluding to the gulf between what we claim to believe in and the reality of American life. Down deep, we don't like being hypocritical, but then and now, Lincoln's words place us in these moral dilemmas. This is not just mere finger-pointing; not just a calling-out; but a call to action:

> "In giving freedom to the slave, we assure
> freedom to the free; honorable alike in what we give
> and what we preserve..."

The *house divided* rhetoric became more than a biblical allusion when the country erupted into a war against itself. The cataclysm of the Civil War served as an ordeal of fire.

> "Now we are engaged in a great civil war,
> testing whether that nation, or any nation
> so conceived and so dedicated can long endure."

The horrible suffering and loss of life in the Civil War was beyond the comprehension of even the wisest among us. No one could have predicted the depth and breadth of this tragedy. In his Second Inaugural Address — *the other speech*-- Lincoln sounded like an Old Testament prophet, pondering the notion that perhaps America was being punished for 250 years of slavery. However, he had come to see the war as the necessary trial for the nation. He saw the struggle as a fire raging through acres of forest wilderness, only to renew the forest with new growth and new life.

At Gettysburg, Lincoln proposed that the nation have a new birth of freedom. The only way to honor those who died was to complete "the great task remaining before us." There was only one hope to dignify the terrible loss the country had endured, and that was to finish the work of expanding liberty and equality. The blood spilled in the Civil War allowed for a narrowing of the gap, if you will, between the real and the ideal:

> "...the we here highly resolve that these
> dead shall not have died in vain—that this nation,
> under God, shall have a new birth of freedom--
> and that government of the people, by the people
> for the people, shall not perish from the earth."

Lincoln's message goes far beyond the dedication of a cemetery in Pennsylvania. The subtext of the Gettysburg Address resonates through the years as our purpose—our creed. The great task remains: "It is for us the living to be dedicated to the unfinished work..."

And if you work for something; at something; toward something; hard enough and long enough, the work becomes the something.

Some have said that Lincoln waffled on the moral issues of the war. After all he was a politician. Does this erode his position as a leader...as a visionary? I think not. Without compromising where necessary, he would never have been in position to define the great moral dilemmas of his time; perhaps for all time. Lincoln found that at times, in order to bend and persuade others, he had to compromise. Tangible goals could never be reached if he supported high-minded but unachievable aims. He never lost sight of his objective. At times, he only inched toward it; other times, he backed off completely. When the chance did come though, there was no doubt about what needed to be done.

When he said at Gettysburg that words could not add to the actions of men on the battlefield, Lincoln was simply showing his humility. Always raising the message above the messenger, he knew our connection to words...to the idea. His were for all time. They raised the value of my father's service in World War II; heightened the honor of my uncle's deeds in three wars; and deepened the sense of loss of the neighborhood kid in Vietnam.

Lincoln's writings have transformed each succeeding generation. His words reveal a higher understanding of the human condition, and they have served to steer the course toward a freer, more just world. Perhaps the true strength of Martin Luther King, Jr. was his ability to see his own struggle in the context of Lincoln's. King reminded us of Lincoln's words, and that we are still bound to *finish the work*. By crafting his words to challenge us to pursue the ideal, Abraham Lincoln served the highest purpose of a leader.

It's Good to Know

...driving down the lonely road
Forty seven miles from home
At ten damn thirty on a Thursday night:

As I cross the St. Johns River,
I see a boat offshore —
It's good to know
There are men fishing, tonight.
It's good to know
There are men in taverns,
Perched upon their barstools
Talking politics
And swapping tales of the great Ted Williams.

It's good to know
There are old men sitting in their dens,
Reading —
Dozing off every now and then...
And there are men telling stories to their kids
Then kissing them good night.

As I blast across Route 50
Headed for the coast,
I think back upon a week of work and worry,
And I curse my maddening hurry.
Still it's good to know there are men fishing.

November 24

It's a breezy, cloudy Sunday morning. A cold front is struggling to make its way down the peninsula. It's three quarters through November and Florida has yet to see a day or night in the fifties, but confidence is brimming, you see, that Thanksgiving will bring something resembling a change of seasons. Regardless, Quinn will be up early Thursday smoking the turkey and pork roast. Actually, it's more like Wednesday night. The cooking starts around midnight.

When the kids were young, they would wake up with him every few hours to check the coals. In the morning he'd make a fire in the fireplace, no matter the weather, and his daughter would be right in front of it, watching the parade on TV. To be honest, his role was not very labor intensive. His wife spent most of the morning in the kitchen as he stood watch over the smoker, making the near seamless transition from hot coffee to cold beer.

Quinn has lived in this place all of his life. He and Jean were born and raised in this once sleepy coastal town. But this is Florida and traditions are the results of regional, cultural and spiritual minglings. They ate early on Thanksgiving as Southern families do. And they would gather again for leftovers on Friday…then a bonfire awaited; accompanied by funny stories told over and over again. Each dish served at the feast was a recipe from grandparents, aunts and uncles, and friends. However, no tradition was more important than smoking that turkey. His grandfather had taught him all he knew about this turkey business. Gramps was the king of outdoor cooking—grilling, rotisserie, smoking; you name it. At any one time, he was known to have three to four cookers lined up on his back porch.

In passing the torch to his sons and grandsons, Gramps did what he could with limited skills—*coaching 'em up*, as the head ball coach would say. His great grandson, however had the "grilling bug." He pulled up the other day with a smoker so big it needed a license tag.

Gramps would arrive early to check on the cooking progress and share a few refreshments. The look of pure joy on his face when sampling the turkey was a sight to behold. Through the years, there were many talks around the smokers and the grills. Regardless of the occasion, they would gather there around the fire. No deep conversations, mind you, just talk of the beauty of evening or the necessity of cooking steaks right down on the coals. *"Don't let your fire get too hot, son…and cook 'em right down on the coals."*

We males are a curious lot. We often grapple with expressing our feelings. Quinn and his own father spoke to each other in code. It was a love expressed through the language of sports. Gramps spoke to his boys around the barbeque. In his later years, when his health was failing, he felt it necessary to talk openly about his feelings. It seemed he wanted nothing left unsaid. Quinn sort of wished he hadn't done that. He already knew.

Gramps has been gone now several years, but Quinn can still hear his gentle drawl when he fires up the smoker. On Thursday evening, after all the football games are over, and when everyone has come and gone, he'll sneak an extra piece of pie, with a slice of pork or turkey on the side, and remember. Happy Thanksgiving.

Stories To Tell

"Be suspicious of all motives, even your own."
-Christopher Hitchens

If my goal is to tell the story of America; and why it has a unique place in the history of civilization, then there are indispensible chapters in that story…chapters I cannot condense; parts I cannot revise; things I can't skip for the purpose of spending more time and energy elsewhere. I cannot and will not jump to contemporary events that seem fresher and somehow more relevant to modern life.

For the record, I want to teach as much as I know…I don't want to leave any of it out. It's all significant. But no modern story is more relevant than Jefferson's; or Anne Hutchinson's; or Lincoln's. How can I not tell the story of Andrew Jackson? Or of Sam Houston?

How can a person fully grasp the resolve in the hearts of men at Gettysburg and Normandy if she doesn't know the hearts of men? How can we even begin to understand the price they're willing to pay fighting our enemies in Afghanistan or wildfires in California? What are they fighting for? Is it not the American Idea, found deep in their love for family, friends, sweethearts, cities and towns? There we find Jefferson's pursuit of happiness…not as some floating abstraction…but as something new and fresh in each and every one of their stories…all of our stories. It's timeless. This is the mythology of America.

The relevance, the connection between generations is a personal one. When it comes down to it, we all want the same things. At first glance, it seems easier to connect with those in somewhat similar circumstances, but it's not necessarily situations and circumstances that link us. Our needs, desires, strengths, and weaknesses are also ties that bind.

We race along on some linear progression, moving further and further away from the Idea, as if time and distance do us part. We use tiresome phrases like "stuck in the past" and "life got in the way," as if our history was a place other than here. Faulkner said the past is never gone, it's not even past.

Common Core, the latest education reform, requires High School History teachers to skim over the beginnings of America and focus on more recent events. We are reassured that the essentials of early American History have been "covered" in the Middle School curriculum. *Whew! What a relief...one less thing to worry about...*

The box has been checked. America the Idea has been addressed in the eighth grade, so let's move on. Forgive the sarcasm, but it appears that our approach to education often resembles a to-do list. *Okay, got that one out of the way, what's next?*

I don't know if I can teach a single lesson without at least indirectly referring to Jefferson and Lincoln. If Wendell Wilkie is right, and American liberty is in fact a religion, then how can American History be taught without frequent repetition of its Creed? It's not just another theme, it's *the* theme, and it must permeate every lesson:

- *How did Lincoln transform the Declaration into a Creed?*
- *Did these policies bolster or weaken the Creed?*
- *How did JFK and Reagan use the Creed?*
- *What was Martin Luther King's role in strengthening the Creed?*
- *How is FDR's Four Freedoms speech related to the Creed?*
- *How do these actions reflect the Creed?*

We cannot skip the fundamentals any more than Math or Science teachers can. *Common Core* seems to be a nice, marketable term, but if we called it *Crucial Core,* maybe educators would feel a greater burden of responsibility for the curriculum, and stop trying to fix what's not broken.

One of the more tedious tasks of the American History teacher is to compel students to look behind the curtain, so to speak. It's a tough chore to teach them to check primary sources; to look at the agendas of historians; and to evaluate causes and effects. The hazard lies in the fact that students may often miss the richness of the stories.

Advanced Placement students generally struggle with the *American Pageant* textbook because it's a narrative. They become so used to examining and evaluating sources that they forgot how to discover the plot, as Shelby Foote reminded us. They often complain because a narrative history makes their detective work more difficult. It's a delicate balance we strive to achieve. Ideally, a history student is part detective and part explorer.

Unfortunately, most textbooks don't follow Bailey's lead (*American Pageant*). Most authors have fallen victim to the pressure of lowering the bar. *How can we make this more appealing…more relevant? How can we make it easier?* The result is the texts become thinner and more colorful. The major weakness is not what they put in the book, but what they leave out. I remind my students that just as history's characters are flawed, so are history's story tellers.

December 8

Monday morning…first hint of light…unseasonably warm, even for Florida. Quinn stood gazing upward at the quarter moon…the last quarter.

The moon reminded him of mornings in the Keys when they would troll through Tavernier Creek to get to open water. It took them nearly half an hour to wind through the mangroves at idle speed. The boys rigged the lines and checked the workings of the boat while Quinn stood on the bow of his Mako staring at the horizon, waiting for the first sliver of sunrise. Quinn was never a very good fisherman, but he was a lucky one, and as he got older he enjoyed the boating trips as much as the fishing. The boys were all grown now — married with kids. It became harder and harder for them all to get together…but every chance they got, they headed for blue water.

It had been a two-book weekend. He had spent much of the time recovering from a cold, switching back and forth between David Warner's *Vanishing Florida* and *White Guilt* by Shelby Steele. Actually, the latter was a reread; a powerful reassessment of the Civil Rights movement through the eyes of a former militant activist. Warner's book, on the other hand, was a unique guide through seldom heard-of parts of his beloved home state.

After the dogs had their fill of the yard, Quinn brought them inside and sat down at the table by the window to write for a while before he got ready for work. Like most mornings, when he stepped out of the shower and over the brown dog, he was again filled with great expectancy; mindful of Louis L'Amour's premise that life can be divided into anticipation and memory. After all these years in the classroom, Quinn still felt that rush of anticipation…he was in the business of stoking memories.

There had been so many times when he had locked the door at the end of the day feeling so low he thought he couldn't right himself. He had failed so miserably, maybe he shouldn't even come back. But morning would come just the same, and he would drink his coffee and greet the day with high hopes. He never figured out how he could be so deciduous about his profession and survive. He did feel a sense of risk though, in writing about the workings of his passion, for he didn't want to disturb something so close to his being.

Despite his optimism, morning classes did not go smoothly. In fact they were lousy....three interruptions including a fire drill. Quinn thought it would be a good day to go outside and spend his planning period reading...it was a beautiful December day.

As he approached the green bench with his Cuban sandwich and cup of lukewarm coffee, Quinn could see that a young woman was already sitting down, sipping a smoothie.

"You're late," she said cheerfully.

"Story of my life," Quinn replied. He was surprised to see her again. He placed his book beside him on the bench and opened up his sandwich. She picked up the book and leafed through it, reading the title out loud, "*Returning to Earth by* Jim Harrison. You're rough on a book...ever hear of a book mark?"

"Good Afternoon, Ms. Richardson, how are you?" He was relieved he remembered her name.

"Fair, Mr. Quinn, fair. And what does Jim Harrison have to say on this fine day?"

"Well, quite a bit, actually," he answered. "Ravens and crows aren't just ravens and crows."

"Hmmm." Jodi feigned interest. Again she leafed through the pages of Quinn's book. The spaces between the scars of dog-ears told of short and erratic reading intervals.

"The reading habits of a man can say a lot about him," she said.

Quinn had no comeback.

"So, Mr. Quinn, you never answered my question the last time I was down here."

"That's the second time you called me that. Mr. Quinn?" he repeated. "Hell, the kids don't even call me that anymore."

"What do they call you then?" Jodi asked.

"Just Quinn. I prefer 'Captain,' but it's just Quinn."

Jodi smiled. "So Mr. Quinn; my question…"

"You're going to have to let me think about that," It had been a long morning.

"I thought sure you would have a prepared spiel," Jodi said.

Quinn shook his head and a smile came to his face. "I guess I'm notorious for that."

> *The times demand you feel the future bearing down,*
> *But I have nothing but the past to wrap my arms around.*

"Who wrote that?" she asked.

"Me," he replied.

> *A flood of mixed emotions keep the heart at bay*
> *For all your endings and beginnings are tangled up today.*

"Pretty impressive, reciting poetry to a girl and it's just our second date," Jodi said, playfully elbowing Quinn in the ribs.

"I'm old, but I ain't dead," Quinn responded. They both laughed.

His mood lightened.

"I can't imagine doing something I don't love," he said. "But love can be torturous. What about you, do you love it?"

"I asked first," she said.

"Well," said Quinn, "I'll give it a think."

Quinn started eating his sandwich. He tried to shift the conversation. "So, where'd you go to school?"

"Flagler," she answered.

"Oh, St. Augustine, one of my favorite towns," he said.

"That's right…history guy," said Jodi.

"Yeah, and a bar guy…there's a little place called the Milltop. The Milltop Tavern and Listening Room…right down on St. George Street…cold beer…guy with a guitar…view of the fort and the Matanzas River."

"A little 'divey,' don't you think," Jodi replied.

"Absolutely," Quinn said, talking with his mouth full.

"So, Ms. Richardson, what did Flagler College teach you about Faulkner?" His wheels were turning now.

"A little."

"I once had students who were direct descendants of William Faulkner…two sisters, wonderful girls."

Jodi seemed impressed. *"The past is never gone,"* she said.

"It's not even past." Quinn finished the quote.

"So much of history is bad news," she said after a moment.

"So much news is bad news. No triumph without tribulation," Quinn answered, but the dissatisfaction with his own remark made him squirm.

Jodi seemed amused. "Oh, is that like no guts, no glory? No pain, no gain?"

Quinn laughed, then sighed. "I guess it's the cost of knowing versus the cost of not knowing. Believe me, I struggle with that every day."

Jodi sat back, crossed her arms, and listened.

"I think the notion that the past is palpable in the here and now greatly affects the way we live. When we disregard the past, it blinds us to seeing the value of today."

"Whew!" she said.

Quinn went on. "I wrote an essay once. Actually, it became a sermon for my students. It sort of took on a life of its own."

"I'm listening," she said.

"We were doing a lesson on Mel Fisher," Quinn continued. "And his search for Spanish treasure down in the Keys. It turned into an analogy of youth and time, and carpe diem. *Today's the day,* the old man would say. *Today we find the treasure.* You know, there used to be a history teacher over at Hoover who was a treasure hunter…Jack Deppner…great story teller. He preached *seize the day* long before I ever figured it out."

"Dead Poets Society,"

"Yeah," he said. "Now that was a great movie…I have a picture of Robin Williams in my classroom."

"I thought every day of teaching would be like that," Jodi said, playing with the straw in her smoothie. "I would be inspiring my students…Carpe Diem!"

Quinn smiled and waved to a passing student. "Well, I'm not sure my experience had anything to do with the movie, but it was definitely an epiphany. It came upon my boat while chasing a sunset through the Gulf of Mexico. Have you ever seen a sunset on the Gulf after a storm? It will take your breath away!" Quinn gave her little time to answer and for some reason he was standing now, so Jodi put her feet up on the bench.

"We had been out all morning. The weather turned bad around noon, and I mean bad…waterspout-dodging bad. We spent the rest of the day ducking in and out of the intracoastal, but on the way back on the outside, the water laid down…coke bottle green, and the Creator put on a show. I've never been the same."

"I think I'd like to read that essay if you don't mind," Jodi said.

Quinn laughed as the bell rang. "My, I can go on and on. The guy with us on that day, he was a good good friend, but we lost touch somehow." Quinn sighed at the cost of remembering.

"Thank you for that, Mr. Quinn, and the poetry," she said, heading for the stairs.

The American Idea
On Self-Determination

Drifting out, a mile or two offshore
That's where I like to be.
The tide pulls, the wind pushes;
The currents guide;
But no man drives me.

How's the saying go? "Freedom is not Free." I understand the sentiment: Freedom is precious; it's fragile; it's vulnerable; it's fleeting; and it's very costly. But what is this freedom? Why is it so important? It sent me back to bookshelves.

Now you may think we stepped into a huge philosophical debate—that the answers to such questions are wide and varied, but actually our Founders were quite specific. Liberty is not an end, but a means. It is not an effect, but a cause. It's not a destination but a road to be traveled.

My own mind is my own church, Paine would say.
I'm the captain of my search — out and away!

It's always been like this;
At the core of every creed, a democratic seed:
The individual — Unobstructed
By dogma and social organization.
Solely responsible for his or her salvation.

Now I could use a few prophets
I don't know about you.
Maybe a Christian. Hindu.
Muslim or Jew.
Still, I've got to be my own priest
On this journey down to become the very least.
Out and away. Out, down, and away.

Liberty is more than just the absence of restraint, it's the freedom to explore and discover; to build and create; and perhaps most importantly, liberty implies that each individual is guided by a conscience — an inner voice.[20] We must see our liberty as something more than the absence of restraint. Surely that unbridled feeling of my youth is there inside me, and I hope I never lose it, but it's more.

America rests on the belief that the individual is responsible for his own spiritual state. Thomas Jefferson and his fellows believed that the purpose of freedom was to allow each and every one of us to discover our own way. The First Amendment states, "Congress shall make no law respecting the establishment of religion or restricting the free exercise thereof…" This was not necessarily meant to create a secular America. It was intended to protect against existing forms and institutions which obstruct or divert or constrain the individual's search for truth and purpose. *Discovery is the act of finding something unexpectedly. Maybe we aren't even searching in the first place, but as we live unfettered, we just might stumble upon something.* Freedom then, is a spiritual idea.

We're on our own, then.
On our own, but not alone.
Can truth be found alone?
In the commerce of ideas;
In books and songs and conversations;
In both our travels and our habitations, we may find it.

In barbershops; at bus stops; and exchanges over countertops.
What we stumble on in pubs
Or 'round the kitchen table;
Without doctrine. Without party. Without label.

The free market of the mind
Challenges the orthodox, leaving certitude behind!

If only we can stay uncaptured;
Unbridled by greed
Unblinded by the mortal need.
Unconquered by oppression, whatever its disguise;
Yet still driven to find purpose without compromise.

---

[20]Needleman, 148.

As Jefferson was a product of the Enlightenment, so was the American Idea. He railed against any organization or institution that
obstructed individual freedom. The goal was not merely liberty for liberty's sake. In fact, it was believed to be the very purpose of a democratic society.

Hemingway said boil it down,
Don't spread it thin.
Liberty insists that truth and meaning
Must be found within.
She's stubborn on that point.

Like his contemporaries, Jefferson believed it to be the right of every person to make choices about how to lead his life. In order to find meaning, the individual must begin with an identity independent of social relations and situations.[21] Although we've been warned away from the metaphysical, and scholars are careful to sidestep philosophical notions of democracy, at the very core of self-determination lay great philosophical questions. Those questions have giant political implications, and in the case of America, such questions may well define "the experiment." Democracy is philosophical in its very nature, and freedom then is not a goal in itself, but a necessary precondition for pursuing that which is judged valuable.[22] Democratic individuality is fostered within an environment free of oppression and degradation; absent of exclusion and enclosure. This of course, **is** the Idea. It's why Thoreau went to the woods.

People came here.
Not coming to, but getting out of
And away from…
There.
The degradation, oppression and despair.
For here, in this place, lives an idea

---

[21] Will Kymlicka., *Contemporary Philosophy—An Introduction* (Oxford: Clarndon Press, 1990), 208.
[22] Ibid.

That a member of the human race
Can possibly advance
To something higher...something deeper.
Any man or woman, free from all those brimstone rants;
Taking liberty at second glance —
Disenthralled — free in great wide open space,
Can find a sovereign grace.

I believe any understanding of the republic requires a grasp of Emerson and Thoreau...maybe John Muir would help. If democratic government finds its only legitimacy in guaranteeing individual rights, then we should embrace the culture created by this personal liberty. These great nineteenth century writers started peeling back the layers of the onion in order to gain understandings of a rights-based society.

What emerges from their work is a vital sense of connectedness. In discovering the value of his own freedom, one gains an appreciation for the freedom of others. I have a pretty strong understanding of the Constitution, but before I read Thoreau, I never fully understood the centrality of rights in our republic. Individual liberty not only offers legitimacy to a democratic government, it is essential to its functioning. Here, we find "the process" by which a citizen *becomes* the most fundamental element in a democratic society. Majorities and minorities are **not** the most vital factors in the workings of democracy; it is the individual citizen himself who makes it work.

Whether his journey to the woods was literal or figurative, the purpose was the same. In becoming self-reliant — both physically and psychologically independent — the individual acquires a sense of resistance on behalf of others.[23] Thoreau believed that those of us who are safe have an obligation to take risks to help the less fortunate. The individual has a responsibility to make sure others enjoy those rights he himself possesses, but he must arrive at that realization on

---

[23] George Kateb, *Democratic Individuality and the Meaning of Rights.* Nancy Rosenbloom, editor, *Liberalism and the Moral Life* (Cambridge: Harvard University Press, 1989), 193.

his own. When we teach about freedom, we must make students understand that it's a process of discovery rather than a simple static birthright. A student must eventually grasp the fragile nature of rights, and realize how freedoms are interdependent upon others' freedoms.

Is it any wonder that it was Abraham Lincoln—a man from the woods—who so artfully expressed the reciprocal nature of freedom? We often marvel at the fact that Lincoln rose from humble beginnings. Perhaps it's even more important to recognize what he brought with him.

> "As I would not be a slave
> I would not be a master."
> -A. Lincoln

Thoreau urged us to take in the world with appreciation and admiration, but it was that development of a feeling of connectedness—the move past self-concern which makes his work so resonant. Is it possible for Americans to comprehend sacrifice, community, and shared responsibility without first understanding the value of our own liberties? I'm not much of a social engineer, myself, but the proposition here is that there has to be a process by which an individual must stand on his own hind legs before he can become a functional citizen.

Here again, we've stumbled upon the reason why American History is so indispensible, and why **the American story must never be separated from the American Idea.** A lack of understanding of the fundamental American principles can lead to the creation of policies that weaken them. Again, we are reminded that liberty is more than the lack of restraint. Each of us are bound by what Jefferson called an inner voice…a conscience.

If you don't believe in this conscience then we should stop right here. There's no need to go further with this. If you don't think people know what's best for them, then we should fold up the maps and be done with it. Democracy rests on the premise that the individual is responsible for his own fate…his own salvation, as Luther put it. If government becomes the surrogate conscience of individuals; a third party charged with doling out justice and compassion, are we not separating individual liberty from its purpose? By giving government such responsibilities, are we not abdicating our own?

The search for purpose is of course at the very core of education. From the outside looking in, our public school system appears to have gone way beyond secular. Because we are so frightened to offend anyone; so afraid to be provocative or controversial, it seems as if we have sanitized the material for the purpose of arriving at what Jim Harrison called "a harmless product." Even our discussions of freedom leave out the heavy fact that responsibilities and duty go along with it. If students aren't learning the hard truth that liberty is made possible only when individuals are constrained by their own moral codes, then freedom becomes something superficial.

Our story is one of individuals acting out of their own moral sense. In truth, a school is not a camp for the indoctrination of "isms" — progressivism; conservatism; socialism; capitalism; atheism; Christianism; Islamism. An American school exists **not** for the purpose of promoting political and religious dogma, but to pursue something true to Jefferson's vision — to become a marketplace for the free exchange of ideas. At its best, school can be a place where faith and culture and reason bump into each other, and I'm thinking that our discoveries — or most of them — are serendipitous and accidental anyway.

The individual's journey to enlightenment follows an odd pattern in our society. He searches for truth, finds a little, and sometimes expresses it to the world. He must fight the obstructions of political power, religious power, and money power. In his efforts to find truth, the individual must question existing norms and throw off established "isms." But by doing so, he is challenging those that hold power and is summarily condemned as a rebel and heretic for challenging dogma.

If his argument survives, it may well become accepted, and even adopted by the mainstream. Perhaps it becomes a guide for others, but then gradually, it becomes dogma itself; an obstacle to others seeking truth and meaning. So the process begins anew.

But every truth discovered, every meaning found,
The philosophers and pundits build a fence around.
No fences.

In modern society, we are reminded of what happened to Bob Dylan in the tumult of the 1960's. Dylan, a gifted folk musician, was hailed as the spokesman of his generation. When he resisted that role, he was stalked and harassed for years. Dylan was challenged to come out and take charge and lead the people. Everywhere he turned, he was implored to stop shirking his responsibilities as the "conscience of a generation."

"I would tell them repeatedly that I was not a spokesman
for anybody and that I was only a musician."
-Bob Dylan[24]

Dylan insisted that his number one priority was his family; raising his children with the cherished ideals of freedom and equality. But no one would leave him alone. After all these years people are still showing up at his house, pleading with him to show them the
way.[25]

Of course the irony of all this is that Dylan was being co-opted by those who saw themselves as standing up to the Establishment. In their blind passion, they were unwittingly creating a new establishment or dogma; one that will possess rigid new rules as it will become an institution itself. The New Left. Dylan, to this day, will have none of it.

There is some degree of good news in this process: each generation, the rebels keep showing up. The brainwashers must start their work over and over again, and as Bruce Chatwin said. "this, in the end, is a very wearisome business."[26]

---

[24]
Bob Dylan, *Chronicle (New York: Simon and Schuster, 2004), 119.*
[25] Ibid.
[26] Bruce Chatwin, *The Songlines (*New York: Penguin Books, 1987), 65.

I'm not exactly sure what Thomas Jefferson would say,
But he did believe that every soul must get up and out   And try
to find his way. Every human is compelled, not just allowed
To cut a path uncharted; to live a life unbowed.

I can't speak for you and I won't.
But before my time is up, I hope to learn some wisdom of the ages;
To fill my cup with the words of children,
Prophets, priests, and sages.

Drifting out, a mile or two off shore,
That's where I like to be.
The tide pulls, the wind pushes,
The currents guide; no man drives me.

But I'm going ashore again to reread Luther,
Dylan, Whitman, and Thoreau.
To chew on words of the greatest thinkers known.
Then I'll go…
go to the woods or back on the boat
And try to find Jesus on my own.

One Day Came

One day came —
Known just by number
Not by name,
One day, now broken.

One day dawned…one day came down
But somehow not here and gone —
It keeps hanging 'round.

Time has dulled the edges —
And tempered by the fire,
we pretend to heal;
Again, we chase
our hungers and desires —

Ain't that America, says the Indiana man —
But as we try to understand;
as we sit and fret,
I can't help but think
that we lament the loss
Of something deeper yet.

And like an old river,
We take the path of least resistance,
All the while not knowing where it leads.
Cutting through the clay,
Meandering through the grass and reeds.
On this wayless way,
We satisfy the mortal needs;
But all the getting and the spending
Cannot keep us safe and warm
And write the happy ending.

There is a gulf between us and our creed
That sends one back to bookshelves,
Searching for a wisdom we can heed.
The New Englander is there to say
What it is exactly
He thinks is missing on this day;
It is ourselves that we withhold which dims the light.
We must give the gift outright…

Now, Lincoln said it best –
Just pass the Declaration's test:
Believe that crazy proposition
That we're born free and equal,
And you walk with Jefferson!

But there are three hundred million of us!
We spend our days, apart –
Attending to our habits of the heart;
Going our separate ways,
Denying all along every instinct of the herd.
I've got my music--you've got yours
And they tell me we are tied
By some belief
that only living free can bring?
The proverb says it's not the song,
But in the fact we sing!

That deed of gift, said Frost,
is war, however,
And as one day broken
changed us all forever more,
Will it come together,
the way it's never been before?
It may be the story has only just begun.
As in the ancient allegory,
Our eyes adjusted to the sun;
Only now can see what's real.

Though some return to caves,
Preferring shadows on the wall
Confused and overwhelmed
by the fury of it all,
Others find catharsis in the fire…
And once again, the hymn may well have found a choir.
Will this ordeal; this test
Prove the creed is stronger than the steel?

One day dawned…one day came down
   But somehow not here and gone –
   It keeps hanging 'round.

December 16

"You nick my spruce until its fiber cracks
It gives up standing straight and goes down swishing.
You link an arm in its arm and you lean
Across the light snow homeward smelling green..."
-Frost

Quinn repeated the line, "...tree by enterprise and expedition," then closed the book. It was a big test day, but the season required a poem...and a story. He sat down in his rocking chair, and slowly and deliberately he began:

It was our first Christmas together. I was fresh out of college, swinging a hammer for a living and my wife was working at a bank. We rented a little frame house off Melbourne Avenue. Poor but proud, we were determined to make it on our own and very reluctant to ask help from our parents. The house had no heat and it had to be the coldest Florida winter in memory. I'd make a fire in the fireplace at night and we'd roll out the sleeping bag on the hardwood floor--just the three of us. Oh yeah, did I mention our German Shepherd puppy? I do believe she ate better than both of us.

Romantic moments are tempered by hard realities, and things were really tough for us that first year. I remember her getting the blues at the thought of a lean Christmas coming...so lean that a Christmas Tree purchase seemed out of reach. One evening, in an effort to cheer her up, I told her a story about an old tradition my side of the family used to have.

Each December, my father would lead an expedition south of here to cut down an authentic Florida Christmas Tree. We have a sand ridge running along the east coast, and on that ridge lives the Florida short-needle pine...or what we called the sand pine. To us, they are beautiful, but friends, they're not quite the shape of the trees you find at stores. The branches are few and far between; and the shape? Well, as my old man would say, they often looked like a bear ran through them.

To some, this seemed to be a lot of trouble just to capture a homely tree, but my dad would answer the criticism with Robert Frost, saying a store-bought tree is "not the same as tree by enterprise and expedition." Unfortunately, the explosion of growth in central Florida pretty much quashed this tradition. There are houses where there didn't used to be...subdivisions...neighborhoods...fewer and fewer places to find the sand pines.

Nevertheless, I convinced my bride that there was plenty of wide open space south of here; there was surely a place where we could find a tree. Besides, it would be a great adventure. We were tree pirates! Early one Saturday morning, we headed off in the pickup truck. A plan was in place--she would drop me off and I would find a tree, cut it down and await her return. Now to say it went off without a glitch would be something less than the truth. My getaway driver had difficulty finding her way back, and I was stuck in the woods with the contraband, knowing full well the tree police was on my trail! Finally, I heard a blaring horn and a laughing woman. We headed home to decorate our Florida tree, reveling in the one and only heist of our careers. It was not our prettiest tree--I think a bear did run through that one--but it was certainly among our fondest Christmas memories.

The very next year, we started a new tradition that still thrives today--we go buy a tree.

Math, Science,
And Democratic Values

When we gaze upon the gaggle of ethical infants in our nation's capital, we have to ask, "Are these people really the best and brightest our nation has to offer?" "Is this the best we can do?" There is not a statesman among them. If these men and women are products of the American education system, we can only conclude that our educational reforms are going in the wrong direction. Rather than narrowing our focus to the turning out of reliable employees and able consumers, maybe we should try broadening our goal: How about trying to make some productive, responsible humans?

We have to ask ourselves the hard question of why education is important. Is the purpose purely to preserve and promote our economic and military dominance? Don't get me wrong, I like dominance as much as the next guy. But is there something more we're after? The lesson we learn from Washington is that process doesn't matter…"the way" which we do things is irrelevant as long as we reach a goal. How's that bottom-line mentality working for us?

Nearly every study on education; each report by the media; every focus point on reform is on math and science. The social sciences are mentioned merely as an afterthought. Our concerns for reading, writing, and social studies rest upon comfortable statistics derived from standardized tests. Do we assume good citizenship and principled leadership are not important? Or do we think that such things will just naturally rise up out of the streets?

Maybe instead of widening the scope of empirical assessments, we should shift the curriculum toward teaching character and ethics, and do so by tapping into a great resource--our math and science departments. The transition from American History to Physics should be seamless. After all, the Founders were all creatures of the Scientific Revolution, and like all good scientists, they embraced reason, principle, and intellectual integrity — all necessary for our republic to thrive.

What makes a good math teacher (and thus, good math students) is process. He forces you to use the right method to get the right answer... I've heard many a student express frustration with their math or science teacher because even though they arrived at the correct answer, the process was wrong. Exactly. This is also a rock solid ethical lesson for a student: the means justifies the end—not the other way around.

An essential reason for teaching history is to learn conceptions of character. We hear stories of men and women living responsible, courageous, interesting, joyful lives. They can help us make the right choices in our own lives, and so many of them are scientists and mathematicians. Franklin and Jefferson must find their way into our Math and Science classes. It's a perfect fit. As Jefferson had done before him, Abraham Lincoln embraced Euclid and used *The Elements* to prove the absurdity of slavery and the truth of equality.

> "If A. can prove, however conclusively, that he may, of right, enslave B. — why may not B. snatch the same argument, and prove equally, that he may enslave A?– You say A. is white, and B. is black. It is color, then; the lighter, having the right to enslave the darker? Take care. By this rule, you are to be slave to the first man you meet, with a fairer skin than your own. You do not mean color exactly?–You mean the whites are intellectually the superiors of the blacks, and, therefore have the right to enslave them? Take care again. By this rule, you are to be slave to the first man you meet, with an intellect superior to your own. But, say you, it is a question of interest; and, if you can make it your interest, you have the right to enslave another. Very well. And if he can make it his interest, he has the right to enslave you.
>
> –A. Lincoln 1854[27]

---

[27]Quoted in Carl Sandburg, *Abraham Lincoln, The Prairie Years*, 115.

Jefferson on the Porch

I was sitting on the back porch
Pondering Eliot's treason,
Reading just my second book
Of this, the hurricane season.
Again, it dealt with Jefferson – and yet another look
At the mystery of America.

My attention shifted
First, to the brown dog lying at my feet
And then to all my summer chores
That would take me out into the heat.
But then back again to the great Virginian.
Something kept me there in front of the fan
Planted in my seat.

Ah, but the two books I did read that summer were powerful. After finishing Jacob Needleman's *American Soul_*for the second time, I took up Garry Wills' *Inventing America.* I try to read everything Wills writes and as always this one didn't let me down.

In this work, Wills reexamined Jefferson's influences in writing the Declaration of Independence. Contrary to scholarly belief, Wills presented convincing evidence that John Locke was not nearly the political force he has been made out to be. Locke was so admired as a philosopher, that his political views – though not original – were revered also. But Jefferson himself will minimize Locke's influence on the Declaration by linking him with a long line of political thinkers: "All its authority rests on the harmonizing sentiments of the day, whether expressed in conversation, in letters, printed essays, or in the elementary books of public right, as Aristotle, Cicero, Locke, Sidney..."[28]

---

[28] Quoted in Garry Wills, *Inventing America, Jefferson's Declaration of Independence* (New York: Houghton Mifflin, First Mariner Books Edition, 2002), 172.

On that humid morning, I read on –
One more lesson he had to teach;
Of his belief in a moral sense
A benevolence slumbering in each

...Don't need a prophet or a prince, said he,
To tell us right or wrong.
An inner voice – the conscience – it's been here all along!

But Liberty's apostle owned a slave. (or several) (or many)

How could it be
That he was first to write a law to set a people free,
But could not bring himself until the end
To emancipate dear Sally?
A hero? You say now, with the sin that he commits,
He preaches from the pulpit of the hypocrite!
A hero? I say yes. Because he's fallen.

Ah, hypocrisy – Our favorite sin.
And Jefferson knew his crime. He saw it plain.
He smelled the stench and felt the pain.
But if moral contradictions are the measure of a man
Then who is worth a damn among us?

And I've heard others say it:
From the deep and dark recesses
Of our own self-betrayal,
There – the force of moral vision rises.[29]

Perhaps even more important was Wills' claim that Jefferson's philosophy differed dramatically from Locke. Jefferson departed from his contemporaries by embracing "the moral sense" —a conscience— as a separate faculty; believing it to be the basis for all politics and morality.[30]

The terrible irony of Jefferson's philosophy lies in the burdens of his own conscience. By embracing the principles of liberty and equality, while still clinging to the depravity (his word) of slavery, Jefferson wrestled with the moral instinct he claimed exists in all of us. I guess

---

[29] Needleman, 18.
[30] In Wills, *Inventing America, 199.*

it could be said that this conscience allows us to "know" what's right, but it doesn't necessarily compel us to do what's right.

Needleman's work, *The American Soul*, has been a book I've revisited countless times. As I leafed through it again and saw the many margin notes and highlighted phrases, I realized what an impact this book has had upon me. His explanation of the role of heroes and why we need them has greatly influenced my teaching.

If within, there is capacity for good,
Our darkness then, won't be denied.
Man's two natures, rightly understood,
Can't live side by side
But in some constant fight.

I do believe the ancient Greeks may well have had it right —
Long before the Virginian, they tried to understand
The curious forces in the making of a man.
Others said this, too;
Their myths were metaphors of human nature
And the battles that ensue.

The Age's optimism broke with a red sky
And dawn went down to day.
Still, the ghosts of Hobbes and Calvin loom;
How then do we keep our wickedness at bay?

We are violent and corrupt, we are selfish; we are weak.
Wealth and power, we boldly, blindly seek.
Disorderly, chaotic,
Contentious, and profane.
It's clear enough, we have to be constrained.

But we're joyful and creative,
Filled with verse and song.
We are selfless and forgiving,
Compassionate and strong!
And we must have the right
To find a life worth living.
...free to find our way along.

But Of all the philosophical stunts,
How can we be bound and free at once?

Needleman believed that it was essential to see heroes for what they really were: flawed characters filled with
weaknesses and doubt, "but in each of them another greater force existed"[31]

It took me a while to figure out what was going on in all of those Greek tragedies. They were just giving us some lessons on human behavior. Each hero's story represented a great struggle between our two natures. In each case, a great strength collided with a great weakness or unwinnable circumstance.

For generations, American heroes represented that dual nature — the stories of Washington, Jefferson, and Lincoln were stories of men overcoming obstacles and transcending flaws. Unfortunately, over the past few decades, we've done our best to kill our heroes. It seems we're guilty of focusing on stories of only one side of their nature. The American hero is either regarded as a superhuman figure with unattainable virtue and no value to our lives, or as a deeply flawed, overrated hypocrite with little or no relevance.

Old Locke won't take it quite this far,
Insisting we're inventions of the world…
"waxen shapes we are!"
Tabula Rasa…created not within, but out.
There seems little room in him for doubt!
And volumes have been written — taken down and passed along as fact;
That only on self-interest do we truly act.

Now then, a debt is owed to Locke — "Newton of the mind"
His books impress my friends, sitting there upon my shelf.
But the only motive he can find
Is that which benefits oneself?

Where's the moral sense?
The pleasure gained by helping others?
No need to come to Jefferson's defense.

---

[31]Needleman,11.

Like the Scot before him,
Our beleaguered founder – enlightened pioneer
Believed there is no place for determinism, here.

In Calvin, Locke, or Freud,
Whatever the disguise,
With dogma comes iron fetters.
Try on your own free will for size!

"When I do good, I feel good," Lincoln said
His simple creed rings true;
Man and woman must awaken to
What Jefferson already knew:
There's got to be benevolence
In the happiness we doggedly pursue…
…even if we never catch up with it…

Either way, the heroes stand in park as statues, with shoulders adorned with pigeon shit.

In his discussion of heroes, Needleman alluded to the Greek notion. Although humans are dark, selfish, and contentious, they have the power to do good. Needleman believed that heroes and myths play an indispensible role in the American story, but the mythic must include both the real and the ideal. Once again, it comes back to human nature.[32]

Locke's claim that the mind was a blank slate, and his insistence that humans must respond in certain ways rubbed Jefferson the wrong way. Locke's theory that we're all simply products of pleasure and pain challenged the existence of the moral sense[33] . Of course then, his contention that humans can only respond in predictable ways undermines the notion of free will.

Francis Hutcheson *was a Scottish-Irish philosopher who became known as one of the founding fathers of the Scottish Enlightenment.*

---

[32] Needleman, 13.

[33] Wills, *Inventing America,* 183.

January 16

"It's when I'm weary of considerations, And
life is too much like a pathless wood…

…I'd like to get away from earth awhile…"

Cool January morning… test day…he pulled *the Poetry of Robert Frost* from the shelf and flipped to page 121. Today seemed like a good day to read *Birches* to his class. Quinn prefaced the poem by telling of his own tree-climbing youth here in Florida and the joy he found in it.

"When I see birches bend to left and right
Across the lines of straighter darker trees,
I like to think some boy's been swinging them."

After reading several lines, he closed the book and returned to his story. Quinn talked of how his father would gather the kids around a bonfire in the backyard and read them Robert Frost.

He and his sisters were all Florida-born and the poems were his father's way of taking them back deep into his native New England woods. Quinn's mother, a native Floridian herself, had fallen for this Yankee, and it took her cracker fisherman father a long time to get over it. But he eventually did. As they grew up and raised kids of their own, Quinn and his sisters held on to this strange connection they had made with Frost.

"So was I once myself a swinger of birches.
And so I dream of going back to be."

Their memories did not include swinging birch trees, but they had Australian pines. They were tall dark trees planted by farmers to protect their groves from the hurricanes. The trees did their job, perhaps too well, growing so thick a boy adept at climbing could easily swing from one to another.

Quinn told of a time when he helped a neighbor move…the sad chore of leaving her husband. While he was in Daytona enjoying the Firecracker 400, she was packing up. She was an older woman who had doted on his children and he felt obligated to help her out of a bad situation. There were three birch logs she kept on her hearth for decoration, and Quinn noticed them each time he passed. When she offered payment for his help, he refused but reluctantly asked her for the logs. She promised him the birches, but they were somehow lost in the chaos of moving.

Quinn's plan was to give them to his sister, but all that was left was the poem. For Christmas that year, he sent her a verse he had written about the memory.

One morning before Christmas, he awoke to the sight of a river birch sapling planted in his front yard.

Songlines

The Bushmen of Australia to this very day
Believe the world was sung into creation.
They claim we follow songlines
On what seems to be a wayless way.
Can this be true? Who am I to say;
One who named his brown dog a prophet.
We walk and wander, though,
Humming; whistling; singing to ourselves…
Four mile an hour pace;
A four-beat rhythm to our step
In our search for sense of place.
But how's the saying go?
In our trek through time and space, the road is walking too.

I first heard the term in a song by Jimmy Buffett, and that led me to explore Bruce Chatwin's book. He captured me with his explanation of the role songlines played in the cultural history of Australian aborigines.

As I grew older, I began to see how song connects us to place and people and things. Not only do ballads chronicle the past, but the rhythms and melodies also bind us together and   link us to a strange but common history. We begin to see links in the chain.

The original songlines served to guide the wanderer in the footprints of his ancestors. With a four-mile an hour walking pace and a four-beat rhythm to his song, he encountered landmarks and sacred places which kept him on the line to his destination. Our lines seem blurred today, only visible when looking back through memory. But it is the music that conjures up the vision of our pathways.

There's a songline
Weaving through the mangroves
From an old piano out on Cabbage Key;
With words of validation and redemption
In stories shared by friends and family.

Reaching back to Boston, Massachusetts
Through harmonica
And weatherworn guitar.
There are voices spanning generations
Hardened by the rum and good cigars.

The City of New Orleans, Steve Goodman's wonderful song reminds us on that southbound odyssey that movement is comforting, and music somehow reaches down and touches something within us. Perhaps it takes us back to our beginnings, when moving soothed us and left us feeling less vulnerable. There is an instinct among mothers and grandmothers to pick up their children and console them with a soft song and a rocking chair. I can hear my wife's voice as she rocks away anything that could possibly ail my granddaughters.

"…mothers with their babies sweet
rocking to the gentle beat,
and the rhythm of the rails is all they feel."
-Steve Goodman

As I travel through my time here, I've become mindful of Shelby Foote's claim that each life takes on the form of a work of art…a narrative, if you will, and musical in nature. It reaches back from an Irish Catholic immigrant causing trouble for the steel mills of western Pennsylvania, to a cabin on the side of a North Carolina mountain; back to a woman born to a Key West fisherman in the 1930's, who would bear a daughter with whom I would fall in love and marry.

…from a rough tavern in Pittsburgh — *Jimmy's Place* — where my father sowed his seeds long before I came along…through the den of an old Florida Cracker who was the most learned man I've ever known. As a boy, I would sit and listen to his songlines connecting his soul with his space, and in turn, awakening mine.

The links of chain to you and me
Are found in Lincoln's mystic chords of memory.
From the churches and the taverns;
To the front steps down the street
Where the bluesman sits alone
And plays the saxophone so sweet.

Through all of this, a mysterious stream of music reached to the core. From the bagpipes calling from my ancestry; and that first Dylan song I heard; from those rowdy evenings in the pub singing Irish rebel songs, or sitting in the dark listening to Kris Kristofferson; to that first Bob Marley tape I played over and over again on my boat. "Old Pirates yes they rob I," sang the old Floridian. "Sold I to the merchant ships." I guess we can all use a redemption song.

Searching for songlines is an occupation which leads us deeper within ourselves. It changes the way we look at knowledge; at philosophy; at the world itself.

> *There's a songline*
> *Running through Savannah.*
> *I hear it stretches down to Florida Bay!*
> *Or maybe all the way to old Havana;*
> *We'll find it on some bright September day.*
>
> *But there's a squall line*
> *That spans the intracoastal.*
> *Lightning flashes cut across the sky.*
> *The blowing rain jabs my skin like needles,*
> *But the echoes of the music hold me by.*
> *Oh, there's an old tune*
> *That plays out on the salt air*
> *From a boom box bungeed to the bow.*
> *Many travels; few destinations,*
> *But the memories that I visit lift me now.*
>
> *Like a sunset I remember off Shell Island*
> *And a moonrise I recall on Melbourne Beach.*
> *There are children laughing in the rain out in my driveway.*
> *There are moments we're beyond the mortal reach.*
>
> *There's a songline*
> *Running through Sebastian*
> *From an old piano out on Cabbage Key;*
> *With thoughts of home*
> *Before the Great Migration*
> *In stories shared by friends and family.*

Reaching back to Pittsburgh, Pennsylvania
And from Irish pubs
With old men raising jars.
There are voices spanning every ocean
Sweetened by the beer and good cigars.

How does this connect to my students? Well, that's a long and winding road. Early on in my career, I got into the habit of putting a quote on the board each day. It was usually something thoughtful or insightful, sometimes humorous. Oftentimes it pertained to the lesson in some way. Bob Potter, a good friend and colleague of mine, got a real kick out of my daily ritual. He would sometimes slip into my room before school and put his own version of wisdom on my board. It would be a phrase from a popular song or some hilarious Zen verse he made up on the fly. Bob kept things in perspective.

His fun, however, had an unintended outcome (my favorite kind). I began to mix up the sources for my thoughts of the day. Along with Turkish proverbs, Emily Dickinson, and Mark Twain, came lines from musicians like John Prine, Janis Joplin and of course, Dylan. The quotes were often maxims or mottos, but sometimes, they were simply phrases—lines I may have heard on my way to work.

No one knew just what to expect when they walked in and looked up at the board each day. One time, it would be Galileo or Gandhi, followed the next day by John Mellencamp, Keith Richards, or Dave Matthews. Alice Walker made her appearances; not to be outdone by Bruce Springsteen, Woody Guthrie, and Dorothy Parker. Students are creatures of habit, and I could tell something was sticking when I'd forget to change the quote for a day or two, and a normally shy kid would speak up with indignation. Some would ask to bring in their own quotes. A few of those are now in my collection (thanks, Holly, Alyse...Kait...).

The words of the day evolved into songs of the day. For years, we started school at 7:15, and it's hard to get kids rolling that early. I started jacking them up with music as they came in each day. The Allman Brothers' *Blue Skies* was one of my favorites. It was better than coffee. Tom Petty, Jimmy Buffett, and course, the Rolling Stones reared their heads.

The choice of music changed throughout the day depending on circumstances, and my mood. Buffett was there to sing us through hurricane season. And we had to play the Blues on Monday. Heavens.

The ritual took on a larger role than I ever planned, especially for some of those kids who were slightly less than motivated. It's disturbing to see a student's eyes void of expectation. It is exhilarating to see that change. Some were awakened to the possibilities by the music. Many had never heard Bob Dylan or Merle Haggard. Bob Marley now sang accompaniment as they completed their assignment.

"Without music," Nietzsche said, "life would be a mistake."

I try to work music into my lessons at every turn. I give them primers on the different genres; my musicians in class would school us all on technical aspects. I try to put music into historical context — Jazz as a form of social protest; Folk as a means of social action. But I also remind them that music is always there just to make us feel good.

Of course, music rituals became music projects. Those started when I was teaching a Sociology class years ago, and struggling to make it the least bit interesting. Nothing screams party like Emile Durkheim. I was trying to explain the relevance of cultural diffusion and failing at it. Coincidentally , we were studying the Roaring Twenties in History class, and I stumbled upon Ken Burns' documentary on Jazz. The light went on as soon as I heard Wynton Marsalis liken Jazz to gumbo. The next day, *Project Music* was born.

I had heard Tom Petty say one time that all roads led back to Dylan, and I heard Dylan himself insist that everything goes back to Woody Guthrie and Muddy Waters. Now I had a plan.

The format of the project was backwards. Students chose one of their favorite artists and would present a biography of that artist, including a description of their style or genre. An essential requirement of the biography was to identify three musical influences on their artist. My directions were specific: Who was your artist listening to when he or she was your age? That requirement wasn't too difficult of a challenge. Artists love to talk about their roots.

The projects really took off.   Many students did elaborate presentations—posters, videos, and slideshows. It wasn't long before we started hearing the names of people they had heard on my stereo. Somewhere along the way, the assignment crossed over from Sociology into my History classes.

A month or two later, we did Part Two, presenting *the influences on their influences.* Each road did seem to lead back through Elvis and Dylan; through Woody Guthrie, Leadbelly, and Muddy Watters; back to Son House, and Robert Johnson at the crossroads. My Country music fans were amazed to discover how Hank Williams and Jimmie Rodgers combined Folk and Blues to invent country music. I tried to take them farther back; back to the Scots-Irish immigrants; back to Jefferson playing the fiddle while writing the Declaration of Independence.

Let's be honest. This doesn't work for everybody. I have my annual quota of kids who think "this is lame." Each class would have the usual number of sleepy ones standing up in front with a wrinkled piece of notebook paper on which they had hastily drawn an epic music flow chart. They get their laughs and then sit down. I feel bad for them, but we move on. "There are," as Lincoln said and I love to repeat, "some fleas a dog can't reach."

 Project Music took on a life of its own. Guitars started showing up in my classroom. Kids I thought were painfully shy were now sitting in front of the class singing Dylan.

The administration frowned upon the possession of guitars on campus. Even the most well-meaning students were told to pack them up when they were caught playing in the hallway before school or during lunch. I started giving them asylum in my classroom, telling them not to worry, that it was just the remnants of the Red Scare. None of us knew what the hell that meant.

There's something subversive about a guitar, but also very democratic. I like to tell the story of Woody Guthrie borrowing a bumper-sticker reading, "This Machine Kills Fascists" from GI's in World War II. Soldiers would put them on their tanks. Woody slapped one on his guitar.

Although their brave recitals would often slow me down, I could not refuse a student's request to play in front of the class. Those wooden boxes strung with wire became a source of empowerment.

> But through all that I have witnessed;
> And in the wonders I've been blessed
> To discover and explore,
> There is music that connects us--that reaches to the core.

January 27

Monday had been a perfectly awful day. Only seven out of 29 students chose to do a class project. Quinn was furious, and he cut a broad swath with his anger. It was usually a pretty popular assignment, a welcome change from the bell to bell lecture and discussion. But this group of upperclassmen had decided that it wasn't worth the effort.

"Candlesnuffers," he called them. "You have no curiosity!" Each day his anger seemed to deepen. "Am I crushed at the thought of failing to motivate you?" "Am I sickened by your total lack of respect for learning?" Quinn refused to let them off the hook. "You don't even think enough of me to lift a finger to pursue an assignment I handed you on a silver platter! The sole purpose was self-gratification, you little mercenaries, and a wee bit of enlightenment."

He simmered for a few days, and just when the seniors thought they were out of the woods, Quinn would strike again: "Instead of Thoreau or Whitman today…rather than Invictus, we'll read a little Eliot" (Quinn changed it up just enough so they knew he was speaking to them).

> *You are the hollow ones, the stuffed ones*
> *Leaning together, your dried voices*
> *When you whisper together are quiet and meaningless*
> *As wind in dry grass*
> *Or rats' feet over broken glass*
> *In your dry cellar…*
> *…Shape without form, shade without color,*
> *paralyzed force, gesture without motion.*
> *…Those who remember (you) –if at all – not as lost violent*
> *souls, but only as the hollow ones, the stuffed ones…*

He closed the book and turned on a movie.

Out and Away

Drifting out, a mile or two offshore
That's where I like to be.
The tide pulls, the wind pushes;
The currents guide;
But no man drives me.

My own mind is my own church, Tom Paine would say.
I'm the captain of my search — out and away!

Now I could use a few prophets,
I don't know about you.
Maybe a Christian. Hindu.
Muslim or Jew.
Still, I've got to be my own priest
On this journey down to become the very least.
Out and away. Out, down, and away.

Last time I set my feet on land
I bought myself a pair of shoes
And headed in to listen
To the reverend preach the news.
But on the street outside, I heard a saxophone wailing.
I found myself wandering down
To sit on steps with an old Black man
Who tried to make me understand
That God is all around.
"Please play," I say.
"Play the blues so we don't have the blues."
"Got to get 'em out, Irishman," he says. *"Out and away."*

Drifting out, a mile or two offshore
The tide pulls, the wind pushes;
The currents guide…

Jackie and Jim

Know your song well…

If you ever met my sister and brother-in-law, Jackie and Jim Lepper, you would know why I so graciously accept the honor of being the third best history teacher in my family. They are my mentors. They inspired me to go into the profession, and I do covet that bronze medal. "Jackie and Jim." It's difficult to speak of one without the other—both so fiercely independent, so unique, yet somehow better together than they could ever be apart. They are among the most authentic individuals I've known.

Walking into their house was like following the footprints of my ancestry. The Early American décor was diffused with all things Irish. It was filled with artifacts and treasures—paintings and pictures; busts of Lincoln and Shakespeare. Music. There was always music. And books.

The back den was dark and earthy, often lit by a single lamp and a fire from the Franklin stove. The front room, facing east, was bright and airy; earning the name "White O'Morn" (remembering John Ford's *Quiet Man*). There was always the smell of something cooking. Through the years I became rather notorious for the timing of my visits. I'd fall off the radar for a month or so, but then I'd drop in, usually around suppertime, pure coincidence of course. The warmth of welcome was always there; food and grog aplenty, and much, much more.

Oftentimes, above the music, was the sound of spirited political debate, into which I would somehow fall. Jim would usually be sitting in the front room while Jackie's base of operations was the kitchen. She would walk out with a snack or dessert and rattle off a point of argument, a Florence King quip, or a line from TS Eliot, and then retreat to the kitchen. Maybe retreat is the wrong term. Jim was usually the devil's advocate, but he met his match. Jackie could argue politics more doggedly than anyone I've ever encountered. She had an opinion on everything, and it was an educated one. If you dared to walk into a *conversation* with those two, you better know your stuff, because buddy, you were in the Major Leagues of political debate.

From the beginning, they taught me that I must love my subject more than I love my students. It took me years to realize why that was so vital, but I finally figured it out. Historian Shelby Foote said that you must have an affection for whatever you're talking about for it to have any real meaning.[34] As a boy, I would sit around a bonfire with Jim and he would tell me stories. His eyes would light up as he spoke of Jefferson, Lincoln, Ted Williams, his father, or his grandfather. I remember those stories to this day, and I also remember the raw emotion with which he told them.

I was partial to the old dark den. I often entered through the side door, and there it was in all its glory. There was always the smell of smoke from the Franklin stove. In my Florida family, it mattered little what the weather was like outside. Moods and occasions determined if there was a fire or not. Besides, the old Franklin warmed the heart far better than it ever warmed the room. Now that Jackie is gone, it's hard for me to go back in there, but the memories are so thick, I have to visit from time to time.

Let me tell you about Jackie. She was a remarkable woman. Jackie had to be the most curious person I've ever met. She was absolutely interested in everything.

She was a teacher...wife...mother...sister...grandmother. She ennobled those titles. Jackie could swing a hammer, play piano. fix a leaky faucet, write a poem, paint a portrait, I'm not kidding! Paint a portrait. She could saw a board, play guitar, win a beauty contest, and pan fry the best chicken you ever tasted.

She loved churches...churches and pubs. And gardens. Gardens and humble Irish cottages. Back to the pubs for a minute--

---

[34] Quoted in "Interviews," *Shelby Foote, The Art of Fiction No. 158 (The Paris Review, Summer 1999).* Retrieved from http://www.theparisreview.org/interviews/931/the-art-of-fiction-no-158-shelby-foote

Now I am sure that she liked "the cozy corner," the quaint little place where she could sit with friends and talk a little treason. But deep down, Jackie loved the rowdy ones. Not the fake green beer-swilling, Irish-for-a-night bar. No, she liked the over-crowded- boisterous table- thumping, Guiness-spilling, thatch roof-raising, Irish Rebel song-singing pub. Jackie knew the words to every Irish song.

In their travels in search of fine establishments, Jackie was also quick to find the proximity of the Church. To quote a great philosopher, there's a fine line between Saturday night and Sunday morning! Heck, there she was at a Jimmy Buffett concert, swaying with the lawn people- singing the words to every song. (well maybe not every song). Jackie would tell you, "Jimmy's Irish, you know." Along with Ronald Reagan, Abraham Lincoln, and Bob Marley. *(that's our story...and we're sticking to it)*

Jackie loved Ireland, Savannah, and Gainesville…and long walks through old Melbourne. She loved books. Much to my chagrin, Jackie did not like boats. She did not like pretentious behavior...She did not like....well...This list can go on because if there was something Jackie didn't like, she told you straight up! The News of Nations filled her talk, but the itch for power never afflicted her. Sometimes, I wish it had. No one loved America more than Jackie. There was never a woman—never a person—more qualified for public office. Intelligence, insight, integrity. Poise. And an iron will to do the right thing. She did not pursue public office. Instead , she chose to serve her family, her students, her God. On this path, Jackie served the country she loved tenfold. She was the epitome of the highest position a person can hold in a democracy: CITIZEN.

Jackie's favorite Bob Marley line—oh yes, she quoted him often—was "emancipate yourself from mental slavery." And she practiced that wisdom throughout her life. Jackie believed that true freedom, true dignity, true equality came from within. No rule, no law, no policy, no custom could do for you what you could do for yourself.

Jackie's influence on my teaching was much more spiritual than tangible. We taught in separate spheres, but she led by example. The energy she put into teaching was beyond comparison. She would exhaust herself, to the point of compromising her health. She was the most thoroughly prepared instructor I've known.

"I know my song well before I start singing"
-Bob Dylan

Jim Lepper is not only a mentor, he is one of my heroes. But I don't get Jim for myself. I have to share him with the countless others he has influenced. Whether you've encountered him in the classroom, the playing field, or gym, or you've bellied up to the bar next to him, you have walked away impressed. Jim has a presence that is immediately apparent upon meeting him. There is this humility and good humor, but above all there is integrity...a firm adherence to a code of values that governs the way he acts, the way he works, and the way he treats other people.

I was sitting with Jim in a bar by the marina, enjoying a cold beer and a taking stock of decades of teaching American History. He has since retired from the profession, after forty five stellar years in the classroom, dwarfing both my contributions and my tenure.

"Maybe I'll reinvent myself," I said. "You know, trudge into the twenty-first century; incorporate a few new strategies...some bells and whistles." His answer: "Why in the hell would you want to do that? Do what you do."

But what is it that I do? How would I describe my teaching "style," anyway? Lecture? Conversational lecture? A narrative filled with story-telling and sometimes-pertinent digressions? Through the years I've figured out what works and what doesn't work mostly through trial and error. There are essential ingredients in a lesson that let it fly. There needs to be levity and humor and emotion, but the lesson goes nowhere without command of the subject matter. Jim Lepper taught me that.

Jim had a fearless commitment to his role as an expositor of knowledge. He offered no apologies for his style; no defense for his devotion to the subject matter. Why should he? Throughout four and a half decades in the classroom, Jim fell in and out of vogue with the administration, as they moved from reform to reform. When once he was a maverick, he became a sage; then a maverick again. The funny thing is, Jim never changed a bit. He was still grinding. This fact reveals something about education reforms, don't you think?

Mark Twain said, "Get your facts straight then you can distort them as you please." Jim Lepper said to go ahead and give students as many facts as you can and have faith that they can make connections on their own without you doing it for them. Did he teach dates? Absolutely. "Dates establish sequence, and sequence establishes relationships." In Jim's eyes, the History teacher's job is to help students learn **how to** think, not **what** to think. That is quite democratic, wouldn't you say?

I will tell you, it's easy to steer students toward certain conclusions, but that is a very slippery slope, and it's surely not our job. To resist that temptation to go down the path of least resistance is the great challenge of the History teacher. It's difficult to present information as truthfully as you can and then let them think for themselves. But that's the beauty of it. Will every student be able to discover the plot? No. But why don't we start with high expectations rather than low ones?

Many education reforms are hailed as being somehow more sensitive to student needs than the traditional teaching styles. That is far from the truth. What a student needs and what a student wants are two different things, and making things easier isn't what a student needs. Jim taught me a lesson I use every day in counseling students and advising parents. *If you're not getting it, work harder.* Not many people want to hear that. Most want a short cut. But some have to work harder than others. That's a flat fact. My high school math teacher told me straight up: "If you want to pass, you have to work harder." I did. I even went to work in his orange groves on weekends. That didn't help my math skills, but it built a bond of trust with a good man and broke down barriers between us. For some reason my performance in class improved. I learned to work harder.

Making something easier for the purpose of improving grades and test scores seems rather corrupt, don't you think? Jim Lepper showed much greater respect for his students by challenging them rather than coddling them. There were many students who failed Jim's class. Nevertheless, his philosophy is much more optimistic and positive than public education policies of constantly lowering the bar of achievement. In the eyes of legislatures, school boards, and many parents, failure is not an option. This notion defies reality. As a former baseball player, I will tell you that failure is a part of success. Heaven help the kid who has never failed at anything.

When I talk of heroes in my class, I remind students that we are all ordinary creatures, but we are capable of extraordinary things. Heroes are flawed characters who possess remarkable traits. We need heroes to inspire us to search and find heroic traits within ourselves…in our own characters. Both Jackie and Jim have served that role for me. They inspired me not only to be a teacher, but also to try to be a better man. When he retired, Jim Lepper did so as the most respected teacher in our community. He's still teaching me.

February 12

Quinn pulled out of the cemetery onto US 1 and headed south. The sky was a clear blue and the temperature was falling, but he had the windows rolled down in the truck. He thought about stopping by *Captain Katanna's* on the river. Quinn could usually find his friend Doug standing at the bar, swapping stories with other locals. Most perched themselves upon their stools, but Doug always stood. He smiled at the image of the man…a good man.

He needed something to change his mood and wash away the afternoon. Instead of running the boat like he had planned, he found himself sitting at the grave of his grandson. Quinn wasn't much of a cemetery man, even with all the loved and lost who rested there, but time and again he came and sat, remembering that precious boy who cried once and then was gone. He never held him.

Rather than stopping at the bar, Quinn decided to swing by the house, pick up the dogs, and drive *the loop.* That was the name he gave for a blues-curing ritual drive south. The *loop* took him down A1A, past Sebastian Inlet, all the way to Wabasso. He would cross the Indian River and head back north on US 1, through Roseland, Micco, and Grant. By the time he got back to Melbourne, things always seemed better.

Sometimes, the excursion had slight delays, to accommodate stops at Sebastian Beach Inn, Honest Johns, or Hiram's. Other times it required a swim in the ocean…usually with the dogs. But today was a straight drive. It was cooling off quickly, and Quinn thought to put on a hoodie when he picked up his companions. Since the windows had to be down so the two could have their heads out at all times, the ride could get a little chilly.

Dave Matthews played over the wind rushing into the cab. Quinn thought how *Crush* would have been a great song in any era. He mentioned that to the dogs and neither seemed to disagree.

It was about 25 miles to Orchid Island, the midpoint of the drive. His favorite part of the trip was the bridge over the Inlet. Traffic was usually light, and Quinn would slow to a crawl at the top of the bridge and gaze out at the ocean and then westward, back at his beloved lagoon. The dogs would whine in anticipation at the sight of the water, hoping for a dip.

As he cruised into Indian River County, the barrier island became a narrow neck of land for a stretch—barely 200 yards wide. Unfortunately, things got rather densely populated as he continued south. The word had long since gotten out about the beauty of this place, and even Disney had staked a claim to resort living. Quinn wondered out loud, "What part of *barrier island* do they not understand?" Even after all of the hurricanes over the past decade, folks were still flocking down to the coast. It did bother him though, that time and again, his tax dollars were used to replenish the sand on the residents' oceanfront property. That didn't make sense. To Quinn, these coastal squatters had lost the frontier spirit.

He turned west and crossed the Indian River over the Wabasso Causeway. The sky was a brilliant orange. Quinn said a little prayer of thanks for the Creator's handiwork. The road wound back to US 1, where he made a right and headed toward Melbourne. The last of the sun was dropping over the trees and as it got colder, the dogs gave up their window and curled up on the back seat. Quinn rolled up the windows, changed the CD, and let Willie Nelson sing them home.

Flags of our Children

"And that Flag is my father"
-Shelby Strother

It may come as a surprise to some folks, but I like the Pledge of Allegiance. Yeah, I may have some libertarian leanings, but I like the Pledge and I love the Flag. Some may wonder how a child of the 60's and 70's emerged as a chest-thumping patriot. My formative political experiences included assassinations, scandals, and riots. I am far removed from the hawk, and the dove for that matter, but my favorite song is still *The Star Spangled Banner*.

(A Pirate Looks at 40 and *Freebird* are close behind.)

All sorts of people have objections to saying the Pledge of Allegiance, and predictably, school boards steer clear of anything controversial. I ask my students to stand, although they have the option not to. In 30 years, I can only remember a few instances where they chose to sit. That's a story for another time.

I'm not quite sure why the Pledge causes such a stir. It's not binding. It doesn't hold you to something you don't want to be held to. The standing is more important than the saying.

I've never been much for taking oaths, or signing codes or pledges. Hell, if you have no loyalty, what good is taking an oath? Anyone can raise their right hand and say it. If you have no honor, what good does it serve to sign an honor code? People without honor would sign anything. The promise must come from within. But there's something about putting my hand over my heart. It reminds me of the spiritual nature of liberty. In its simplest form, a ritual is defined as an act in which one experiences the sacred. What could be a better way to start the day?

Some of the words and phrases in the Pledge — to this day, I'm not sure why they're in there. And maybe the word *allegiance* throws people off. I try to keep my focus on the Flag. But then there's that phrase, *for which it stands.* It jumps out at me. There it is: the American Idea. Individualism. Equality.

The Pledge is first person present tense. I tell my students that the time during the Pledge is deeply personal — "By standing and placing your hand over your heart, in front of the Flag; by embracing your own dignity and worth, you are promising to respect yourself, and hold yourself accountable." The Pledge may mean something more, but it certainly isn't anything less.

The Pledge to the Flag is a reminder. When I see the Flag, I see my father and grandfather. I see my friends and former students who lost their lives in service to our country. And I see my mother and sisters, and Alice Paul and Billie Holiday. But I also see my children and grandchildren. You may see something different. "Take from the Pledge what you need," I tell my students. "Those twenty seconds are for you."

When the Supreme Court ruled flag-burning was *symbolic free speech* (Texas v. Johnson, '89), I think it made a mistake. The Flag is more than a symbol, and even then, symbols hold much more importance than the Court may realize. Once again, we seem to be in the business of cherry-picking the meaning of symbols, largely because we don't know the whole story behind them. Symbols are powerful; they stir passion and sometimes anger. But the Court's act of diminishing the importance of symbols — especially the Flag--serves no lasting purpose in a democracy. Maybe we should stop looking only to lawyers to define our rights, since the question of liberty is not a legal issue but a moral one.

Through all of this, it's still hard as hell to stir patriotism in teenagers. They are so self-conscious, and deathly afraid of appearing cheesy or corny. Even a group of Advanced Placement seniors seem hesitant to let their hair down and express their love of country. "Disenthrall yourself," I'd say, conjuring Lincoln.

But 9/11 changed all that. At least for a while. In the days that followed the attack, we all showed a little more of ourselves to each other. During those dark times, I was given my most memorable day as a teacher.

In my old windowless classroom, a massive 48-star American Flag covered the wall. With all due respect to Alaska and Hawaii, this was the Flag that flew when I was born, and my niece thought I would appreciate the vintage Banner as a gift. I surely did. My students — almost all upperclassmen at the time — were impressed by the sheer size of the Flag, but few noticed the slightly different configuration of stars.

After 9/11, it seemed like we were all searching for some expression of unity, young and old alike. Things that normally seemed cheesy were not. For a time, we let down our guard.

When President Bush threw his support behind the *Pledge Across America,* many of us embraced that moment for the unity it provided. At 2:00 P.M. Eastern Daylight Time, Friday, October 12, students and teachers in over 100,000 schools stood up and said the Pledge of Allegiance together.

At about five minutes to two, there was a knock on my door. When I opened it, there stood fifty or so kids from my other classes. They asked if it was okay if they came in and pledged to "your big old Flag," as they called it.

Begging the fire marshal's forgiveness, I had around 80 students in that dingy room, facing the Flag and saying the Pledge on that day. The moment passed and the students filed out, returning to their classes. After the bell rang ending the period, I stepped through the back door adjoining the library, found a corner, and broke down.

February 15

Quinn sat on the back porch in front of the fan and sipped a morning beer. It had nothing to do with the mournful voices of Johnny Cash or Kris Kristofferson. Well, that's not completely true. But he had a powerful headache and for some reason he thought the beer would help.

He read very little on the weekend and wrote even less. Sunday morning was weighted down by the remnants of a family squabble stuck in his head. How we piss away our time over mindless bullshit. Donegan, the Chocolate Lab, was sprawled out on the floor ten feet away, while Shadow — Black Dog — was wandering around in the yard somewhere. He thought of how dogs paid no nevermind to such mundane things. "Dogs know what time it is," Quinn said to no one there.

He remembered how they never left his side when he was sick. They seemed to have a particular instinct about such things. And every morning there was sheer joy springing from them. "Every day is Christmas," Quinn liked to say.

Shadow found her way to the screen door, bringing a small stick as a gift, but she seemed only halfway interested in playing. Birdsong broke out suddenly from the ancient oaks and the morning lightened. The pain in his head seemed to lessen and he wondered if the reason was the Christmas dogs, the birds, or the beer.

Quinn checked his phone and there was a text message from Ray: "Beers after the game tomorrow?" Quinn smiled and texted back that he was agreeable, and that he was planning to come to the game anyway. That may well have been a stretch of the truth. He hadn't been to a game yet this season.

Small Town Lament

What place is this?
Where am I now?
Marley said to keep my past somehow,
But it's been buried.

They four-laned the highway, here,
I guess it's been now thirty years
And things have gone to hell and back around.
Businesses are booming — people moving down;
We're running out of water...
...we're running out of town.
And my hands are dirty.

Some locals used to hang out
In the bars on the beach
Talking of a past
That's well beyond our reach.
And they couldn't seem to grasp the meaning
When someone said our hands are dirty.

But others drink alone...because they know.

Gazing off their portico
Beyond a manicured front yard,
Pouring Johnny Walker over ice
To sip and swallow hard.

Because they know and understand
That washing well
Cannot begin to cleanse the stains
For selling off their land
To strip malls and fast food chains.
(Ferguson's never sold out)

And I should say some were driven out
By zoning boards (in bed with investors),
For indeed we've all been had.

And I am at once too bitter and too sad
To offer solace.

Jim Crow was barely gone
When Johnny Evans passed away —
A farmer here for fifty years,
Part of Florida's yesterday.
But someone mentioned, 'shopping mall,'
And dominoes began to fall.

They sold out all good wishes
And sold off all his land.
Then plowed his orange groves under
Like so much contraband.
I know somehow my hands are dirty.

Now, even the bars are gone
Where the locals lamented...
...and there's nothing left
For children to see
As they sit as captives,
To hear the tales from sad old me.

I have no anchor line or mooring,
Just a ballast stone or two,
To avoid the starboard list.
For now somehow
The hermit's justified.
And in their rage,
Hiassen's daft heroes seem quite dignified.

Some would say we've stemmed the tide
Against erosion of the years,
For the fashion of the times decide
We keep our yesterdays like souvenirs.
So go restore a few old buildings
We haven't yet torn down.
Go walk amongst the antique shops
In the quaint old part of town.

Others walk alone…because they knew.

In the shade of Melbourne Avenue
They stroll beneath the ancient oaks.
Turning back the hands of time,
Remembering all the old folks.
When a dollar was a dime.

They knew that this would happen;
And harkening Edmund Burke — their hands are dirty.

Down by the boat ramps on the old lagoon
I stand and stare, waiting for the Hunger moon,
Hearing Van Morrison.

A tourist interrupts me, asking where he could find a good cigar.
A fair question. The moment reminds me of a conversation
I had with a bartender in Jamaica who wasn't into eye contact —
or the times I've walked down Duval Street and the locals
pretend not to notice you, unless they're selling something…or everything.

Nowhere Else in the World...

On Tom McIntyre

I pulled into the Hess station on 192 to fill up my truck before work. When I got out, the guy on the other side of the pump looked over as if he might have recognized me. I looked back for a brief moment. He did look familiar, but as usual, I was running late, so I avoided a conversation by staring mindlessly at the gas pump. The pump was slow and for whatever reason, I began to think back on an old friend, Tom McIntyre, and the first time we met.

There used to be a convenience store at the east end of Mathers Bridge—right on South Patrick Drive. I was gassing up my truck one morning before heading to the construction site, when up walked this burly guy...he walked like he was a man on a mission. He was apparently running an errand for his fellow fishermen...refreshments.

His face was familiar and it finally dawned on me who it was. "Hey, that's the football coach at Mel-High! "

At the time, I had been trying desperately to enter the teaching profession—trying to get my foot in the door. So I figured it probably wouldn't hurt to introduce myself.

Anyone who knows Tom can predict how the conversation went. He put down his refreshments, looked me in the eye and shook my hand...didn't know me from Adam's cat! Tom stood there and talked to me like there was nowhere else in the world he'd rather be.

Now I'm sure his fishing buddies were getting thirsty, but that's how every encounter with Tom was. It was like he could not contain all the good inside him so he had to let it spill out at every turn! He had to leave you with a laugh...a smile...a good feeling. He shook my hand again, then picked up his refreshments and headed back toward Mathers Bridge.

That fall, I was hired. And that was the beginning.

Tom was a friend, role model, and mentor. It is hard to imagine a world without him in it. He was such a great influence on those around him. I can honestly say that I wouldn't be a teacher today without him. His guidance and support helped me and countless others. It was as if he saw things in others that we couldn't even see in ourselves. What a great gift for a teacher and coach to possess. What a gift for anyone to possess.

As the years rolled on, Tom became principal and later Area Superintendent. At every level of responsibility, he handled himself with the utmost integrity. Tom *put himself out there* – he reached out to students, teachers, and members of the community. That's a tough thing to do when you're in a position of authority, but he always pulled it off...usually with a smile! That's not an easy thing to do, especially with rock-headed employees like myself.

The fellow at the Hess station was putting the gas nozzle away and taking his receipt when I turned and said, "Hey, don't we know each other?" It turned out we did…a very long time ago. We stood and talked like there was nowhere else in the world we'd rather be.

February 16

Out beyond the leftfield fence, Quinn stood at the top of the football bleachers, leaning on the railing eating a tangerine. He could see Ray in the third base coach's box, hands on his knees, immersed in the game. Quinn soaked in the sights and sounds of everything around him. He thought about walking down to the dugout but decided against it. To say that he missed baseball would be an understatement, once the game touches you, it never leaves you. It's always there. He could still feel the thrill of chasing a ball down in the gap, dropping down a bunt to start a rally; and that was thirty five years ago. His love for baseball was marrow deep. Quinn needed to get away from coaching for a while but that didn't make it any easier. Attending a game felt odd.

Aside from being a damn good friend, Ray was the perfect guy to work for. He trusted his assistant coaches and gave them free rein in their areas of expertise. When the games started, it was all Donohue, and it was an absolute joy to watch. No one had better instincts. His players loved to play for him — some didn't realize it until they graduated. The dugout was always dotted with alumni who came out to root for the latest group of Bulldogs. Even though Ray was fiery, caustic, and extremely competitive, his players always seemed to have more fun than those on other teams. There was a simple joy about his program that few had seen around the diamond.

Melbourne won 5 to 4, another close one. There was a one word text from Ray on Quinn's phone when he checked it: *Longdoggers*. Quinn walked to his truck and headed across the river to meet Ray. It had been pretty warm over the past few days, but February was returning to Florida. Quinn grabbed his hoodie since they'd be sitting outside. It took Ray a while, so he sat by himself watching a surfing video, drinking a Hatteras Red. Finally, the Gator blue Honda pulled up.

"Can't believe you didn't bunt in the 6th."

"Screw you." The server came out and Ray ordered a Bud and asked for a menu. "So, Francis, what have you been doing all weekend, sitting on your porch talking to dogs?"

"As a matter of fact, I have," Quinn answered.

"Oh, before I forget, we had Joe behind the plate, Friday. He asked about you."

"Really? Joe's a good guy."

"Yeah," said Ray. "One of the few umpires you got along with."

"Oh, and you're Miss Congeniality." The jabs continued. These two could make it an Olympic event. The fact of the matter was Ray's razor sharp sense of humor kept him out of trouble. Umpires couldn't get too mad waiting for one of his patented one-liners.

"So, ready to come back?" Ray asked. He always kept the door open.

Quinn laughed and sipped his beer. "So how's the diet going? I heard you're trying to kick the cholesterol medicine."

"Shut the hell up" Just then, Ray's order of chicken wings and onion rings arrived. "You got no damn room to talk."

Teaching Ideas

"Stay with me." If you spent any length of time around my classroom, you've probably heard that line a time or two. I usually use it when I'm losing my audience. I've been known on occasion to embark upon meandering digressions in order to convey a particular idea or concept to my students. Now I do lose a few from time to time; some are gone, never to be heard from again…figuratively speaking, of course.

It's hard to teach about abstract ideas. Hell, they're not easy to think about, let alone talk about, but to borrow from a good baseball movie, it's supposed to be hard; that's the beauty of it.

I know that I've said this before but I honestly don't know what makes an effective teacher. There must be 50 different ways of doing things. One size surely doesn't fit all. What works one day may not work the next. I don't know much about the science of teaching, or the science of learning for that matter. But I know a few things. I know you have to be willing to gamble. You have to take the risk of boring your students…of not reaching them…of *going over their heads*…of falling flat on your face. I have been there.

There are days when I miss my mark…days when I feel I need to apologize to my students as they leave the classroom! Other days, I am frustrated by their intellectual laziness. But if you're not willing to fail in attempting to teach abstractions — if you're not willing to try to bring ideas to life and discover you've fallen short again and again; well then, where do we go from here?

But if you would indulge me, we can begin, as the Irish say, at the beginning. It may seem like I'm splitting hairs when I insist on calling the course "American History" rather than "US History," but it's more than semantics. The United States is a political expression, while "America" is an idea. If we only consider the US as a nation, then we are no different than any other country. *Well, that's not completely true.* As history proves, nations come and go: Greece, Rome, Persia, Germany, and the USSR, to name a few. It means little that the United States is an economic and military giant. What makes us different?

It has happened before.
Strong men put up a city and got a nation together,
And paid singers to sing and women to warble:
We are the greatest city, nothing like us ever was...
                                                    -Carl Sandburg[35]

Democracy. Not simply as a form of government, but in the sense that American democracy allows us to pursue our own "higher principles" within ourselves.[36] What distinguishes America from other civilizations, as I've said before, is its revolutionary view of human nature.

The concept of democracy which sprang from the Enlightenment is rooted in the belief that humans are flawed creatures, but we have the innate capacity for self-improvement. The individual must discover for himself his purpose; his connection to others; and his own definition of happiness. It's a struggle for each of us. For some, it's been tougher. To a large degree, American History is the story of those struggles. Some scholars believe that the very meaning of America is found in the fight to achieve conditions where each person could freely pursue meaning and truth: economic freedom allows us the means, and personal liberty keeps us free from organizations and institutions that would get in our way.

We Americans are often criticized for being too individualistic; too self-centered, but this is rather odd, since the individual is at the very core of a rights-based democracy. God knows teenagers are mired in superficiality. I take every chance to push them to think deep...if only for a fleeting moment. They are listening more than we may think. Maybe the problem is the over-emphasis of materialism, which is a real symptom of freedom gone astray. Jacob Needleman, like Emerson before him, called materialism "a disease of a mind starved for ideas." Materialism will lead us to despair,

---

[35] Carl Sandburg, Four Preludes on Playthings on the Wind, *Harvest Poems*, *(Orlando: Harcourt Brace & World, 1960), 59.*
[36] Needleman, 9.

Needleman went on to say, for "there is nothing in the physical world which gives us hope."[37]

Don't get me wrong. Material comfort is important. The desire for prosperity has been a driving force in our society. But economic individualism is an American value because it serves as a means and not an end. It's impossible to be free without some degree of economic independence. This is much different in the modern industrial world than it was in Thoreau's time, but it's just as essential.

When Lincoln described America as "the last best hope," what did he mean? Hope for what? More equality? More safety? Less misery? More material comfort? Surely, this place offers hope for all of those things, but is there something else?

As I said, ideas are not easy things to teach. They're never easy to think about or talk about. But if we don't, then life becomes an exercise in superficiality. Education can't always be bells and whistles. We have to push our youth to spend some of that intellectual energy. Again, America is the history of an Idea…a history of human nature. More often than not, we reap great rewards for allowing our reach to exceed our grasp.

---

[37] Needleman, 6.

March 5

A cold front brought a chilly wind to central Florida. Quinn sat down at the table facing the window. It was first light and he didn't want to miss it. Bad timing with a nasty head cold…it played hell with his morning ritual of sitting outside with the dogs to greet the coming day. A myth about Florida is that it never gets cold. The old timers claim that your blood gets thin down here. If you spent any length of time in the wide open spaces—on ballfields; on the water; or out in the marsh—you'll find that the wind blows right through you. But it never stays cold for long. There's always hope that it warms up. Yeah, Florida's a place of imperishable hope.

Quinn spent about an hour at the table writing intensely, but the beauty of the morning was distracting, so he put down his pen, put on his hoodie, and headed outside. The dogs followed religiously.

By the time he got to work, he could feel it warming ever so slightly. It was going to be one of those Chamber of Commerce days. Springtime is what seduces so many people to move to Florida. To Quinn it was beautiful all year round, but the spring was something to behold…"Eighties and sixties…Eighties and sixties," he liked to say standing out on the ball field, taking it all in.

Yeah, Florida was seductive…it offered an escape from the brutal Northern winters, but then you woke up and it was June, and humidity came for breakfast. By the time the hurricane months rolled around—August, September, and October—the air and the heat became one and the same, as Shelby Strother liked to say, and so many new arrivals retreated to the air conditioning, awaiting November's reprieve.

For some reason Quinn loved those still, humid Florida mornings. Nothing moved quickly. He and the dogs would sit on the back porch with a fan stirring the air. It conjured up memories of offshore fishing trips when the water would lay down and there wasn't a breath of breeze. They would troll along at three to five miles an hour, waiting for the mahi to hit their lines.

But this was not going to be one of those days. It had all the makings of a fine breezy March afternoon, and Quinn was planning on getting outside first chance.

He read Masefield's *Sea Fever* to his classes because …well, everybody should get to hear *Sea Fever*. The quote of the day was Emily Dickinson, carefully printed on the whiteboard:

"To live is so startling it leaves little time for anything else "

The lesson was on the Jazz Age and Quinn had stepped into the 21st century with what he thought was a state of the art slide show, but he couldn't bear to close the blinds, being that it was so pretty outside.

Early afternoon found him on his old familiar green bench, eating peanuts and drinking a can of green tea. Just when Quinn began to wonder what happened to the young woman who had made herself so comfortable on his bench, here she came walking slowly down the steps.

"Well, Good Afternoon, Ms. Richardson," he said cheerily. "It's been awhile."

Jodi sat down and said nothing.

Before Quinn could try to say something witty or wise, Jodie spoke. "I'm pregnant."

"Are congratulations in order?" Quinn knew the answer to his dumb ass question before he finished it.

"I'm single and pregnant," she said, looking at his face, waiting for a reaction, but Quinn showed no reaction. He had somehow gotten smarter in the last four seconds.

In an instant, he forgot his celebration of the day. He just gazed straight ahead.

Jodi glanced at the time out of habit and got up to leave.

"It's a pretty day," Quinn said, with all the sensitivity he could muster.

She stopped and sat down again. "So how are your classes?" she asked after a long silence.

"Not bad. I told a semi-funny story about Langston Hughes and *Meg O'Malley's*," he said.

"Can you tell me?"

"Some other time," said Quinn. "How about today we just sit?"

July the Third

Shelby Foote,
A man I hold in high esteem,
Said that William Faulkner said
Every Southern boy can dream;
And visit back inside his head
To that summer afternoon;

Waiting there beneath the shade of ancient trees
Before the charge across that field.
Being all that we could ever care to be —
July the Third, Eighteen Sixty Three.

Freedom and Leadership In Modern America

Kennedy, Reagan, and the Power of Rhetoric

"Too many Americans have lost their way, their will, and their sense of purpose..." This quote didn't come from Jimmy Carter's scolding of the nation for our malaise. It actually came from John Kennedy's acceptance speech in 1960. Like many, Kennedy feared that the material prosperity of the times weakened the country's moral resolve; that the drive for personal gain obscured our public concern. This assessment rings true, even more so today.

The fact is we have created a false definition of freedom. We Americans are now convinced that through the piling up of material goods; by trying to satisfy our insatiable desires; we can each find life, liberty, and happiness. But the independence and liberty we find will not be the light of authentic individuality, or the warmth of a conscience-driven purpose. It will be a shallow egoism fed by self-gratification. We throw the word *freedom* around like it's entitlement or empowerment. It's neither. Materialism has become a surrogate for actual freedom. Where did we go astray? How do we find our way back? And make no mistake, we need to find our way back.

Our time in America is marked by the longing for leadership. If only someone would step up and show us the way. In JFK's last speech, he questioned Americans' will to "assume the burdens of leadership," in the world, but if he saw us today, he may also wonder, if we are actually able *to be led*. What appears to be a crisis of leadership in this country walks hand in hand with the problem of a public that is reluctant to follow.

A society founded upon individual autonomy has also produced alienation, cynicism, and apathy. Modern individualism is producing an impractical way of life. Our society is its own worst enemy, and the splintering that is produced may well lead to the very intolerance and totalitarianism we fear, because such developments are more likely to take place when individuals lack a feeling of shared responsibility.

If the people have lost their way, "let the way itself," Needleman said, "be remembered." Let's go back to the true meaning of words like *freedom* and *equality* so we can see them with renewed clarity.[38]

The notion that a leader can emerge and speak with hard words worth listening to seems far-fetched today. But we need to remember that in our darkest hours they have come forth. Just when it seemed like the wheels were coming off, there was someone who came along. So it has happened. And it can happen again.

Freedom

The American experiment is inherently tied to the notion of individual liberty. American culture has come to revolve around the expansive nature of individual rights. It is commonly believed that such an obsession with personal liberty is essential, so that self-determining individuals can be allowed to choose how to lead their lives. But has this obsession gone too far? Has it undermined other vital components of our political culture, including our sense of community? Have we gone overboard in sanctifying rights without demanding responsibility and duty in return? In essence, we've lost the functional definition of freedom.

Of course, more questions abound--What does the individual "owe" the community? Where do a person's rights submit to the rights of the community? Can self-determination be balanced with community responsibility? Where does community and civic virtue fit in the American political tradition? I'm not sure many people are asking these questions...at least the right people aren't asking them, let alone giving us answers. Let's get the ball rolling by offering up a few.

> "Do not be too moral...aim above morality.
> Be not simply good, be good for something."
> -Thoreau

---

[38] Needleman, 281.

Our freedoms are not goods to be possessed…property to be owned. They are the means by which each person develops an individuality, an Emersonian self-reliance in which each of us becomes aware of our authenticity. The purpose of becoming both economically and psychologically independent is for the individual to discover the blessings of liberty for himself.

A sense of life fostered by individual rights can bring a person a new sense of connectedness…and obligation. In realizing the value of her own freedom, she can acquire a new found appreciation for the rights of others.

This is not a new story. Thoreau and Emerson grappled with the getting and the spending just as we do. When he went to the woods, Thoreau was in effect brushing away the clutter of modern life. There may be more to it, but that was certainly an important part of it. By "fronting only the essential facts of life," and by putting "to rout all that was not life," Thoreau was then able to sense his own freedom and realize his responsibility to the freedom of others.[39]

Whether you go to the woods, float down the river in your boat, or just sit on your back porch, Thoreau thought it necessary to "reduce life to its simplest terms." I'm not sure today if many of us know how to do that. It seems that we seldom go *to* anywhere. Instead, we're just getting *away from* the struggles of daily life. …this is where leadership kicks in. We need to be pointed in the right direction.

It is the job of a leader in a republic to communicate to the people the clear meanings of freedom and independence; to remind them of their responsibilities; to call them to civic duty; to instruct them on the American Idea. If a leader fails to do that; if clear and complete functional definitions are not given; if the Idea is left out or watered down, or as Jacob Needleman said, presented as if the meanings were obvious…as if the understandings go without saying, then freedom rings hollow.

The obvious part about the definition of freedom is the part about doing whatever we damn well please. The part that needs to be

---

[39]Quoted in Kateb, 193.

explained — over and over — deals with the responsibilities and consequences that accompany that freedom. JFK historian Richard Reeves hit the nail on the head when he said that the country must be led by words rather than action. Leadership as an exercise and expression of vision has become more important in the last century because of the growing interdependence of modern society and the increased visibility of presidents through electronic media. Two modern presidents, John Kennedy and Ronald Reagan, have stood on the shoulders of giants to greatly impact the leadership role of the office.

Leadership

During the last seventy-five years, the American presidency has changed in dramatic fashion, and the very root of understanding the role of the office lies in seeing how individual presidents have fulfilled their responsibilities. The modern president's impact on the nation quite often depends on personal leadership qualities. This dates back to the earth-shaking changes in presidential leadership that took place during Franklin D. Roosevelt's administration. [40] FDR's firm conviction that the presidency hinges upon moral leadership greatly influenced both Reagan and Kennedy.

> "That is what this office is — a superb opportunity for reapplying, applying to new conditions, the simple rules of human conduct to which we always go back. Without leadership alert and sensitive to change, we…lose our way."
> -Franklin D. Roosevelt[41]

The grave conditions of the Great Depression and World War II, the use of radio as a medium, and FDR's unique leadership skills, all contributed to the birth of the modern presidency. Roosevelt's personal leadership style of confidence, optimism, and determination inspired the nation to rally from the depths of despair and uncertainty. He not only bonded with the American people in these fireside chats, he *educated* them. FDR discussed the fundamental

---

[40] Fred I. Greenstein, "Toward a Modern Presidency" in *Leadership in the Modern Presidency, ed.* Fred Greenstein (Cambridge: President and Fellows of Harvard College), 2-3.

[41] Quoted in William Leuchtenburg, "Franklin D. Roosevelt: The First Modern President" in *Leadership in the Modern Presidency, ed.* Fred I. Greenstein, 16.

issues of American life more so than most of the other presidents combined.[42]

"Millions of Americans came to view the president
as one who was intimately concerned with their welfare."
-William Leuchtenburg[43]

Franklin Roosevelt was never considered an ideologue, and in fact, he's been described as one of the least ideological presidents in memory. But he did have a philosophy. Critics claim he had no grand design, and perhaps it's fair to say that the New Deal possessed no consistent social and economic doctrines. However, Roosevelt had a sound personal belief system, and although he was never known as a man of deep introspection, there is solid evidence supporting the strength of his values in dealing with the big picture.

The commonly held belief is that FDR's struggle with polio deepened his character and strengthened his commitment to public service. Roosevelt developed an abiding belief in the world of action and service, and since he was free from the shackles of ideology, FDR tried anything and everything to make government more responsible to the people. He was as H.L. Mencken said, "a chameleon on plaid, whose uncanny ability to change hats in midstream made him an extraordinary leader."[44]

The 1960 election gave America another president whose personal leadership qualities impacted the office. John Kennedy's tragically short presidency has shrouded any examination of his actual achievements. In our context, however, Kennedy did indeed contribute to the evolving modern presidency.

Kennedy and Reagan were products of FDR's legacy. Post-World War II prosperity made New Deal liberalism a victim of its own success. 50 million baby boomers will grow up in the most affluent society in history. They will never experience the desperate days of world war and depression. JFK shared a belief that America had lost its edge...its sense of purpose. Prosperity had bred a self-

---

[42] Leuchtenburg, 19.

[43] ibid, 15.

[44] Robert Dallek, *An Unfinished Life, John F. Kennedy 1917-1963* (New York: Little Brown and Company, 2003), 321.

satisfied laziness (malaise, if you will), and many began to question whether such people possessed the resolve to meet domestic and world problems.

Some saw the Twenties happening all over again, but JFK nurtured what his biographer Robert Dallek called "a spirit of inspired realism," seeking to reinvigorate the creed and our sense of national purpose.[45] Kennedy wondered out-loud if we were up to the task. Could a rich, comfortable America stand up to the Russian communist challenge? He couldn't help but ask if we were more purposeful in hard times than in good ones.[46]

From the beginning of his campaign to the last speech he gave, his message was clear. Kennedy's rhetoric was charged with a call to duty; a call to choose public interest over private comfort. He urged the people to "live up to the promise"; "to pay any price" and "meet any hardship." The words he used in his speeches brought to mind something higher, a shared national purpose — "discipline," "commitment, ""sacrifice," and "national fulfillment." The trumpet was summoning and Kennedy was leading the charge.

Kennedy's ability to inspire the masses and to stay in our memories may be in itself the very essence of leadership. In his attempt to challenge the American public, he even conjured up the voice of Abraham Lincoln:

> "In your hands, my fellow citizens, more than mine, will rest the final success or failure of our course."[47]

Within his thousand days in office, Kennedy did not achieve presidential greatness, but he did give us a glimpse of what leadership could be in modern America. JFK captured the meaning and power of rhetoric first laid down by Jefferson and Lincoln. He understood, as FDR did, the importance of inspiring, educating, and challenging the American people. In the modern presidency,

---

[45] Dallek, 321.

[46] Ibid, 274.

[47] Quoted in Richard Reeves, *President Kennedy, Profile in Power* (New York: Touchstone, 1993), 39.

however, the role of communicator had also become a major source of power.[48]

With the advent of television, Kennedy's communication skills took him a step beyond FDR's fireside chats. Kennedy and the people around him realized early on that the charismatic young president could use his speaking skills not only to kindle the nation's idealism, but also to supplant his lack of congressional support with public appeal. In the JFK presidency, there is new meaning given to *the bully pulpit.*

Under Kennedy, television became a major factor in the modern president's ability to lead the nation. The way he conducted live press conferences is an example of how he exploited his own public appeal. Kennedy's quick-wittedness and ability to think on his feet disarmed many of his detractors. In contrast, FDR never endured the pressure of a live press conference, and Reagan was never comfortable fielding press questions. But Reagan would find his own niche and become, as the media dubbed him, *the Great Communicator.*

Did Reagan change the direction of America? Did his rhetoric rekindle smoldering traditional values? Or did he miss a chance to carry the torch? William Muir said, "Philosophical ideas have human consequences, and presidents best govern with philosophy." Reagan's philosophy permeated his presidency, and through that, we can begin to understand the relationship between Americans and their leaders.

---

[48] Samuel Kernel, *Going Public* (Washington DC: CQ Press, 1986),348.

Muir and several others claimed that the goal of the Reagan presidency was to achieve a moral revolution--"affecting the character shaping ideas of the American people."[49] Reagan offered no call for responsibility and accountability. It's true that like JFK, he derived a great deal of his power from going straight to the people, but unlike Kennedy, his message contained no challenge, no call to sacrifice. Kennedy believed that challenge could bring national fulfillment through civic duty.[50] Reagan's vision for the country was not the grand counterrevolution desired by neoconservatives, but one that was rooted in simple idealisms of home and family.

> "We must never forget that no government schemes
> are going to perfect man."
> -Ronald Reagan 1983

> "By spreading bounties, donations,
> and benefits...(the government) has assumed
> the responsibilities of our destinies."
> Ronald Reagan 1964

From the beginning of his ascent to national prominence in 1964, Reagan's message was based on a simple powerful theme--that "centrally administered government tended to weaken a free people's character ."[51] Reagan claimed that the people's self-reliance and capacity for self-government was being stripped by a runaway federal bureaucracy.

Again, the strength of Reagan's leadership was built upon the legacies of Roosevelt and Kennedy, and their abilities to communicate with the public. Not only did he utilize his skills to promote policy, but also to make America feel good about itself again. Ronald Reagan's eternal optimism pervaded his presidency and his unique reliance on the media allowed him to translate abstract ideological claims into powerful images. Deregulation of the economy was sold as "Morning in America." Increases in defense spending became patriotic scenes of America's soldiers.

---

[49]William K. Muir, Jr., "Ronald Reagan: The Primacy of Rhetoric" in Fred I. Greenstein, 262.

[50] Dallek, 321.

[51] Muir in Greenstein, 288.

So what do we have here? Was Reagan's symbolic use of traditional American values merely cynical manipulation? On the contrary, he played upon long-standing preconceived notions of the American Creed—liberty, individualism, equality and capitalism—which have served as the bedrock of our national identity[52] Throughout American history, embracing traditional values has often inspired attacks on the status quo. By representing himself as an outsider, Reagan attacked government as the problem, rather than the solution.

Economic rhetoric seldom strayed from Reagan's social and moral themes. He saw the erosion of economic individualism as a threat to other traditional American values. His rhetoric served a reciprocal purpose: the appeal to the American Creed in order to gather support of policies; with the objective of those policies being to give new energy to the Creed itself. But the constant reminder that government assistance should be a last resort rather than a first resort would be Reagan's enduring contribution.[53]

Parts of the Reagan Revolution were impossible to achieve, but other parts were easy. The huge tax cut was easy because it dealt with giving to the people, and not taking from them. Reagan embraced the plan for the giant tax cut, but he had no stomach for the painful shrinkage of the welfare state. To keep the budget solvent, "it required abruptly severing the umbilical cords of dependency that ran from Washington to every nook and cranny of the nation."[54] Reagan would have none of that. So, half of an economic plan was implemented and a monstrous deficit was created. Reagan came to terms with the role of the central government as a welfare state, but today's conservative movement has not.

[52] Herbert McClosky and John Zaller, *The American Ethos* (Cambridge: Harvard University Press,1984), 4.
[53] Aaron Wildavsky, "A ~~World of Difference—The Public Phi~~losophies and Political Behaviors of Rival American Cultures" in *The New American Political System,* Second Version, ed. Anthony King (Washington DC: The AEI Press, 1990), 290.
[54] David Stockman, *The Triumph of Politics, Why the Reagan Revolution Failed (*New York: Harper and Row, 1986), 11.

Reaganism rested on the belief that if the president boosted public morale, then optimistic Americans would make the most of freedom. When they are optimistic, "they stay in school longer, have more babies, start more businesses..." George Will went on to describe it as the "narcotic of cheerfulness"[55]

The anesthetic effect of Reagan's optimism left its mark on America. It all seems so simple, doesn't it? With a rhetorical flourish, Ronald Wilson Reagan revived the American spirit. Inflation eased, unemployment dissipated, and America regained its military prominence. Everything was new again. Or so it seemed.

> "All lies in jest;
> Still a man hears
> What he wants to hear And
> disregards the rest..."
> -Paul Simon
> from *The Boxer*

Embracing values was effective leadership because that's what people wanted to hear. While touting "the new patriotism," Reagan latched into the words of singer/songwriter, Bruce Springsteen. Springsteen devoted most of his energies to portraying Americans enduring a life of injustice, poverty, and violence. But never mind the real story--that's not the America Americans wanted to see. *Born in the U.S.A.* was a song about a disillusioned Vietnam veteran, but many took it as a fierce patriotic proclamation. The song signals the ascendancy of Springsteen as a pop hero.

Flag waving became commonplace at Springsteen's concerts and it did not take long for Reagan and his advisors to make the connection. In the 1984 campaign, Reagan hailed Springsteen as a messenger of hope and dreams for young Americans. This was another example of the nation believing only about itself what it wanted to believe. Springsteen was perceived by many as a man who stood for brazen patriotism. Did Reagan create this illusion? Actually, he was only partly responsible for such illusions, along with a mass public hungry for things to hold onto.

---

[55] George Will, "Looking Backward at the Gipper" in *Conservatism in America Since 1930, A Reader* (New York: New York University Press, 2003), 362.

The power of rhetoric has its limits. On nearly every issue on which Reagan and the public disagreed, he yielded to public opinion. Even with a partisan Senate, Reagan pursued none of the "social issues"--abortion, women's rights and affirmative action-- which made up his moral agenda.

The Reagan presidency changed through the years, and gradually became a rolling referendum. Reaganism made a shift from hawkishness toward the Soviets to "Trust with Verification; from Social Security cuts to a broad catastrophic health insurance bill..."[56] Reagan's was a presidency which entered with ideology and exited with pragmatism. Americans wanted low taxes, but demanded to keep their entitlements. The result is obvious--big deficit. The deficit seemed to give us a glimpse at the modern American character, bent on living beyond our means. French writer Joseph De Maistre said that every nation gets the government it deserves. Ronald Reagan gave us what we wanted...and perhaps what we deserved.

Looking back, Reagan fell far short of his goal of a Jeffersonian minimalist government. In fact, the federal government got bigger on his watch. Why then is Ronald Wilson Reagan held in such high regard among the people? If the social and economic problems have only intensified in recent years, why is the Reagan era considered one of good feelings? To suggest that Reagan had the power to deflect public attention from his errors and misjudgments seems to be a bit of a reach. If there was a *Teflon phenomenon* — to which nothing stuck-- then it may well have been constructed by the electorate itself. Bob Schiefer concluded, "the public had made up its mind about Ronald Reagan, and no matter what was written or said about him the majority of Americans continued to like and support him."[57] Reagan's leadership, however, was bolstered by the public's longing to have a president they would be proud of.

---

[56] Andrew Sullivan, "Mr. Average" *The New Republic, 16 January 1989, p.20*
[57] Bob Schiefer and Gary Paul Gates, *The Acting President* (New York: E.P. Dutton, 1989), 180.

There was credence in Reagan's words. There is a great need for Americans to hear the values he expressed. Self-reliance and economic individualism are vital ideals, but there was no message of self denial, no call to sacrifice, no vision of shared purpose. We heard nothing of responsibility and public service.

Reagan's proclamations of freedom, though at times inspirational, seem to be superficial anecdotes—reminding me that I love Fourth of July picnics, baseball, fried chicken...or the sight of a beautiful woman. Thank you Mr. President, but I don't think I ever forgot. They're all nice to think about, though. His brimming optimism made us feel good because our love for liberty goes without saying. It is obvious and self-evident. What is not obvious is the real meaning of freedom...the price we must pay for it. That part seemed mysteriously missing from Reagan's message.

Maybe his sermons from the bully pulpit he loved should have built upon that self-evident love of freedom. Perhaps he should have spent more time reminding us of the responsibility that comes along with it.

In Reagan's own lifetime, self-denial and self-sacrifice were sewn into the Creed. Commitment, loyalty, duty, and public service were all pervasive themes for his generation. Why in his own presidency did he not extend those themes to the next generation? There were times, of course, when Reagan praised and honored the heroism of those serving in the military, and he deserves full credit for revitalizing national defense and bringing back the strength and pride in our armed services. But is that the only way to fulfill duty, to pay for freedom?

Stay with me, here. Just as I don't want my priest to make it easy for me; to rationalize; to justify or excuse my behavior, I don't want my president to make it easy by speaking of liberty only as license. I get nothing out of a church experience in which the clergyman accommodates my transgressions. Granted, I would like to be forgiven, but not by whisking away my responsibility. Forgive the analogy, but since Wendell Wilkie did describe American liberty as a religion, I think I'm okay. A president should do more than merely imply or suggest the responsibilities and purpose of freedom. He should call me out, and even if I fall short of his calling, I will know the way.

Reagan's message seemed to be that freedom was in fact something intrinsically valuable, but he never reached for an explanation of its function. He talked often of *the bully pulpit,* but maybe he missed a chance to *educate* the American people as other communicators had done in the past. If freedom is your central theme, it's troubling that you would pass up the opportunity to explain why. Ronald Reagan had a finger on the pulse of the nation. He had a chance, as JFK had, to reinvigorate the ideas of duty, service, and sacrifice. By falling short; by presenting an incomplete definition of freedom, Reagan unwittingly contributed to the growth of a false definition. To repeat Needleman's caveat, freedom loses its power when the essential ingredients of reciprocity and responsibility are left out.

Andrew Sullivan described both FDR's New Deal and Reagan's New Right as essential "corrections." The New Deal provided needed fixes for the problems of industrial capitalism, and after half a century, the New Right proposed that government had gone too far with its intrusions. For decades, Reagan spoke of overreach.

In its purest sense, Reagan's vision was in fact, Jeffersonian. But was he blind to the signs that Kennedy and Carter saw? Could he not see that America had lost its way? Surely, Reagan was the type of leader who could have shown us the way back.

Reagan was fond of Thomas Paine's quote: *We can begin the world all over again.* Herein lies a paradox. The American Idea — the proposition that people are born free and equal — was in fact a rejection of human history. The Founders went beyond the stream of history and built upon human nature. When taken outside of its context, the Paine quote is troubling because two hundred years of American history now serves as validation for the founding principles. Our slow, painful march toward more freedom and less oppression is proof of the imperfect but profound wisdom of the Founders.

One of the stark differences between JFK and Reagan was Kennedy's fearlessness in giving the American public bad news. He didn't shield us from the grim realities or tough challenges for fear that it would crush our hopes. In contrast, Reagan seemed reluctant to give it to us straight. A closer examination of Kennedy's famous inaugural address reveals much more than the sunny optimism of youth. He never promised us a rose garden. We were in a long twilight struggle, and we had to be up to the task. If he was discussing the riots in Oxford, Mississippi or the missiles in Cuba, Kennedy gave it to us straight.

Still, many look back warmly at the Reagan years. For his optimism chased rumors of the Decline away, and restored the belief in America's destiny. Praise has been heaped upon Reagan for having an abiding faith in the American people. Why then did he not trust us with the fact that we again faced a twilight struggle? Why didn't he use that great charisma to excite us about the challenges ahead?

Yes, our time in America has been colored by longing for leadership. The daunting task for such a person — if he or she is out there — is not only to inspire trust, but to extend trust. That man or woman must have the confidence and wherewithal to make tough decisions, and also have the faith to call us out and expect an answer; to awaken the virtue that is alive and well in the American people.

March 27

Saturday morning…cold front came through last night for the first day of Spring Break…temperature in the 50's…Quinn savored the chill, thinking it would probably be the last cool air to reach Florida, but you could never really know…

He sat on the porch in the orange slide rocker, writing and listening to Joe Cocker's cover of *The Weight*. His brown dog laid across his feet while Shadow, the young female, stalked squirrels in the yard. Quinn leafed through his notebook and stopped at a Shakespeare quote;

> *And this our life*
> *exempt from public haunt,*
> *finds tongues in trees, books in running brooks,*
> *sermons in stones,*
> *And good in everything. I would not change it*

As You Like It, he remembered. "Yeah…as I like it…"

Quinn knew the water would be choppy so he thought it would be a good idea to leave the boat on the trailer today, and clean it and ready it for what he hoped would be a busy spring and summer. So he got up, poured himself another cup of coffee, and went outside.

The Mako was a bit rough, and it needed new canvas; the gelcoat was oxidized and had some spider cracks; and the teak was faded. But the Evinrude 225 was in great shape, and it would get that old hull up on a plane quicker than you could say Jackie Robinson. Quinn had repowered the boat in '05 in the middle of the housing bubble, when refinancing seemed like stealing. Of course, it wasn't, and now he owed more on the house than it was worth. He took solace in an old Paul Simon line he sang often to himself: *… it's alright. We can't be forever blessed.*

He loved the family excursions down the intracoastal to the spoils islands between Melbourne and Sebastian. The dogs romped along the sandbar, chasing birds and fetching sticks of driftwood. But Quinn also cherished the mornings alone, when he would put in at

Ballard Park and just take the boat north or south, whichever moved him.

As he would turn into the channel and catch the first scent of salt air, it was a religious experience. He felt strangely fortunate not to live right on the lagoon. "No waterfront property for me," he liked to tell Ray. "I don't wanna start taking it for granted."

"You're an idiot," was his buddy's reply. "And you can't afford it anyway."

Quinn's dad often said that there were poems he chose not to commit to memory, because memorization somehow dulled the edges. Quinn likened it to his love of the water. He feared his senses would be dulled to the sights, smells, and sounds if the proximity made it commonplace.

Nevertheless, the oak trees made keeping the boat clean a tough chore. As he scrubbed to the sounds of Bob Marley, he remembered that glorious day when he and his son found the boat...a 1985 Mako 224. It was in Aubundale, way over in the middle of the state. Calvin was the name of the guy who sold it to him and it was not the happiest of occasions for old Calvin. He was waist deep in remodeling his house and apparently running short of cash. He spent little time singing the praises of the boat, unable to hide the remorse he felt over having to sell it.

Calvin stood watching sullenly as they hitched up the Mako. His wife stood next to him, gently rubbing his back...a faint smile came to her face. The last thing he said as they pulled out of the yard was, "This boat catches fish!" And he was right.

Just as Quinn finished rinsing off the inside, Donnegan jumped up into the boat, muddy paws and all. Quinn just stared at him and then shook his head and smiled. Brown dog was taking no chances. He was not about to let the boat leave the yard without him. Quinn faked irritation and told him to get his ass down. He squirted off the boat again and checked his phone. There was a two-word text from **Ray**: Nat's game?

Quinn: Sounds good

Ray: I'll come by around noon

Quinn: Good deal

They had been talking about catching a Spring Training game for a month and here it was, time for the teams to break camp and head north, and neither had made a game. Quinn finished his boat work and then went in to get a shower. Ray pulled up around 12. Quinn apologized to the dogs for leaving and headed out. "They'll be other days, dogs, other days." Ray took US 1 north rather than the Interstate, giving Quinn glimpses of the intracoastal. "Other days," he said again, to himself as he looked out of the window.

Holding Out

For all my graduates...

The first time that we met
I don't specifically recall—
Now, your pictures hang immortal
There upon my wall.

I saw you without vision
And you saw me just as blind
But castle building is no occupation
For the narrow mind.

Staring out with folded arms
More frightened than you know
Trading style for substance
Passing grit for show.

You there in your world;
Me, way out here in mine—
The road between us, serpentine.

And here you are--dressing up
And drinking from the blessing cup
At this your rite of passage.

Sentimental words must not play down
This ritual celebration in your graduation gown.

So please forgive this quaint indulgence
Before the future flies—
For holding on is easier
Than saying our goodbyes

I'm sure you wonder how
But you survived the preaching.
So you endure it now—
Just a little longer:
Behold what has not killed you yet

Must make you all the stronger!

Some say history is dead.
Hush now, children, don't you fret,
Robert Nesta Marley said
We can't forget
For the sake of some bright future.
Island songs give spirits lift
And yet, we wonder why we drift.
The rhythm moves us on this day
But rhyme and reason seem so far away.

You've heard buckets of philosophy
And principle and policy
But where is the grand design, you say.
You've heard the call to duty
And moral obligation,
But what are the ties that bind, today?
Where is this America?

The phone rings, the door knocks,
The voice beckons
From the television set;
Constantly reminding us
Of our eternal debt

Reaching out for something
That we cannot comprehend
Universal Family
And the brotherhood of men.

But Thoreau said, **Free yourself!**
From what the neighbors say;
And only then, you start
To reap the harvest of sweet liberty
From the habits of your heart.

So you must be an island, then
Unto your family and your friends.
You must tend to your own garden…

...finding your connection
To the brotherhood of men.

Go march to your own drummer
But if you follow or you lead,
May your conscience hold you prisoner
And serve the captive's need.

May those friends and family
Be the best things that you know
May you feel the sanctity
Of holding on and letting go.

But **holding out,** you see,
That is indeed the toughest test.
To stand your ground
And do your level best
To keep your **youth unbound!**
To nurture deep inside you
The spirit of the child
To try to keep alive within
What is magic...what is wild.

Take a drive down A-1-A
And leave your worries there
Roll down all the windows
Let the wind blow through your hair
Play the music loud
And smell the ocean air.

Climb atop a mountain ridge
In the coolness of the dawn.
Reach through the fog for sunlight
Then scream and carry on!

Find yourself a front porch
With a hammock or a swing
Take the time to read...
...take the time to sing.
These are my hopes for you

As you move on through the years
May you whisper poetry into your children's ears.
Hold them tightly to your breast
And calm their greatest fears…
…and your own…

Not above you, nor beyond you
But beside you now I stand
Beneath the witness tree.
It's time for you to climb
But return someday to tell me
what you see.

Some things I feel about you are so difficult to say
Big words, insisted Ernest Hemingway,
Don't tell big emotion—
We've known this all the while.
And for this your graduation ,
I leave you with a smile…And an end…to all my rambling…

To J.B.

I pulled the record from the shelf
To settle here and soothe myself
With Buffett's tunes.
Acoustic guitar and subtle hint
Of harmonica and mandolin
Can take me away…can bring me back
To some familiar spot within.

To a time before some changes came around
And put me in my place.

"fragrance on the pillowcase"
Conjures up a name and faded memory
Of a young girl's face;
It was from some distant Florida June
Beneath the spell of a quarter moon.

Album jacket notes from '73,
The maiden voyage to the Keys—
A grasp of his philosophy, perhaps.

So here's to an old friend I've never met
Whose images grow clearer yet
As both of us get older.

Blessed are the Offended

On Picasso, Liberty, and the Confederate Flag

There's a story I remember hearing about Frederick Douglass. I've told it so many times that, as John Prine would say, the memory is worn. Details are sketchy, but as I remember it, it was one of Douglass' last public appearances. He stood at the podium for a moment and said nothing. Then, in one spurt, he delivered his whole speech: "Agitate. Agitate. Agitate." With one word, Douglass captured the essence of free expression. There has to be an edge to the free exchange of ideas and opinions.

As time goes by, we seem to have become more and more easily offended. We stand in righteous indignation at the slightest insult, the smallest transgression. Maybe it's not that we're so thin-skinned, but that our reactions to offenses are so disproportionate to the act. Any remark or action that seems the least bit insensitive or inappropriate is condemned as a systemic obstacle to justice and tranquility. It is seen as a symptom of something much more troublesome. Our policy is simple: *when in doubt, ban it!* It appears that we're bent on achieving what Hitchens liked to call a state of blissed-out ignorance. But you don't do battle with things in history by erasing them. "Cleansing history of things that bring us discomfort," Clay Travis said, "isn't what free societies hoping to learn from the past do."

Should the Confederate Flag be flown at the foot of the South Carolina capital? Probably not, in any context. But this attack, this attempt to remove things from history that we dislike; that make us feel uncomfortable, is dangerous. It's Huxley-like. *Whisk — and those specks of antique dirt all were gone…* Just as the director of *Selma* did to the memory of LBJ — all his deeds were whisked away. Whatever your view of them, at least the Sons of Confederate Veterans have a connection to the past. They embrace history. My dad told me of some brutal experiences he had in World War II, even today it makes me squirm. But I will tell my children those stories…and my grandchildren.

Context. Our inability or unwillingness to grasp the complexities of history blinds us to context. That flag means different things to different people, but our desire to boil down issues to simple explanations won't allow us to see that. Was the Civil War caused by slavery? Yes. But it takes a whole semester to explain that. It's complicated, and well it should be...human nature is complicated. Was Lincoln against slavery? Yes, with every bone in his body. But could he save the Union by initially making it a war to free slaves? No.

85% of White Southerners owned no slaves, but they would never have been called to arms had it not been for the issue of slavery. They would not have had to defend their states, or worse yet, they wouldn't have had to march across that field in Pennsylvania. The clouded issues of the 1860's make our ancestors deeds no less heroic, and their courage is worthy of remembrance. When I see the Confederate flag, I don't see the Edmund Pettus Bridge in 1965 and those segregationists who hijacked the flag. Wait a minute, I do see them or I wouldn't have mentioned them. Oh yeah, another context.

You know, on second thought, maybe I do want to offend you...a free man or woman must have the capacity to be insulted. These days, I'm often frustrated in my attempts to call out my students; to question their character to appeal to their pride; my rants just bead off of them like water off a duck's back. They are quick to ask me what's wrong—why am I in a bad mood? My intensity is construed as grumpiness...and I explain to them over and over that democratic citizens must learn to be annoyed, irritated, agitated. "If you're not pissed off about something," I tell them, "then you're obviously not paying attention." Now if you spend all of your time in that state then you're not going to be invited to many parties. It's important to choose your battles or you'll end up like Thomas Paine, sitting at the end of the bar alone. The Irish have always been good at balancing their political and social affairs. The trouble with the Irish, my dad liked to say, is that we'd head down to the pub to talk a little treason and have such a damn good time we forgot what we were pissed about.

In my slightly warped view of the world, I like to think of the Confederate flag in yet another context. It also serves as a reminder of what happens when the power elite start drumming up causes for war. "States' Rights," they called it—a concept that even Jefferson and Madison briefly embraced. It always seems to rear its head at the wrong time for the wrong reason. I explored the idea extensively in my Master's thesis and I've come to believe that centralization is in fact a threat to democracy. Much of my work was devoted to showing how the power of states has been eroded by the expanding role of the national government. Throughout American History, however, States Rights is often defended by those elites who fear the loss of their position. Yeah, a figleaf, as Florence King would say, to conceal their desires to keep political and economic power. And over 600,000 Americans lost their lives because of it. As my professor said, "there are good reasons and real reasons."

I firmly believe that many or most of the Southerners were fighting to protect their states, their towns, and their homes. But that is not why they were dragged into this war. Ironically, just as the Civil War destroyed slavery, it will also mortally wound the 10th Amendment—States Rights. That flag should remind us of such things.

So, in all its tangled complexity, we cannot stoop to intellectual laziness and cherry-pick our causes and effects. This stems from our lack of appreciation and understanding of history. The fact that both sides of any historical argument pull things out of context is proof of our national amnesia. We don't get to keep parts of America...we get all of it. We're stuck with the whole package. Along with the Prophet Lincoln, we get his depression and ...his crazy wife. Families get the drunk uncle along with everybody else. And even if we have a limited knowledge of the past, if we grasp the essential truth that the story is always a complicated one. Then we can use what we do know to understand America as a natural struggle of human nature.

Artists are some of the most fervent defenders of our freedom. Painters, writers, poets, and musicians all possess a clear eye on human nature and what Kennedy called a sensitivity for justice. Picasso believed that both "art and liberty, like the fire of Prometheus, are things one must steal."[58] There's always something subversive about freedom. We should remember that, and embrace the adolescent sense of getting away with something. Picasso didn't want his art to be simply decorative—something to hang over your couch. He wanted it to punch you in the stomach.

One of his most acclaimed works was *Guernica*. It's a massive mural—over 11 feet tall and 25 feet wide—depicting the brutal bombing of a village in northern Spain by German warplanes. The mural is disturbing. It shows the horrible destruction and suffering caused by the attack in particular and war in general.

So the story goes that while living in Paris during the Nazi occupation, Picasso was approached by a German officer who after seeing a photo of *Guernica*, asked him, "Did you make this mess?" Picasso replied, "No, you did."

It's not only the artist and activist who stand up for liberty. I always try to remind my students of how pirates, cowboys, and musicians are defenders of individualism and freedom. Jefferson himself opposed any institution that was an obstacle to individuality. Throughout American history, the rogues, mavericks, and outlaws have personified the bare naked notion of liberty. We should be very careful about even considering banning or censoring anything. The agitators, the instigators, and the offenders may well be our best protectors.

---

[58] Quoted in George Seldes, *The Great Thoughts,* (New York: Ballantine Books, 1985), 330.

We Can Do No Great Things

On some September Sunday
In a pastel dawn, he sat upon the sand
Leafing through his thoughts on
The measure of a man.

Restless member of the human race —
He runs his fingers
Through his thinning hair
And down the lines upon his face;
Where does he fit? What is his place?
Will he disappear without a trace?
Disregarding Edmund Burke,
He bears the weight of his life's work.

And his faith serves not to comfort him
But to beat and batter.
For within, there lies the burning need
To make a mark;
The haunting drive to matter…
And on this fine day,
All good will — all good wishes wash away.

Words reach out from memory —
Something Eliot wrote,
Of private treasons
One commits for mortal needs —
Doing rightful deeds
For wrongful reasons!

He wonders how
He can toss this all aside.
Can he find the strength
To throw off self-importance —
To cast off vanity and pride?

Standing now, he opens up his wallet
And there beneath a wrinkled ten,
He finds a faded, folded page;
Creased and crumpled; worn with age —
There, scribed as verse with a fine point pen,
He reads the lines of a saint again.

The words of Mother Teresa:

> *We can do no great things.*
> *Just small things with great love.*

It was a message given by a faithful one
Who saw beneath his thin veneer.
Who hoped somehow that he
Would someday see
What was to her so very clear.

Faith again served not to comfort
But disturb
And bring the man a tear;
For therein lies the mystery
And in the mystery rests the beauty
And the fear.

We can do no great things.
We can do no great things.
Just small things with great love.

And this — this was perhaps
As hopes abound, a push; a shove,
From God above; from God within;
From God right here and all around.

April 8

"You know, Jodi, it's probably not a great idea for you to be seen hanging around me," Quinn said.

"That was a bullshit thing to say, Mr. Quinn."

"Are you sure you're not Irish?" Quinn was amused by her reaction.

"Yeah," she said, "and I've been on a roll with my career moves, lately. What, are you some sort of pariah?"

"Maybe the price we pay for speaking out or standing up is always higher than we anticipate," said Quinn with a philosophical tone in his voice.

"So, Mr. Quinn, are you a…rogue…a contrarian?" she asked.

"Good choice of words," he said. "Hitchens said that claiming the title of dissident requires a degree of sacrifice, and I'm not sure I like the price I've had to pay through the years."

"Like…?"

"Sometimes you get treated differently. Maybe you get held at arm's length," Quinn replied. "Maybe your reputation hits the room before you do. I get the impression sometimes that people around here think I live a life of conflict and confrontation…that I'm constantly at war."

"Well aren't you? I mean, why did you think I came down here in the first place?" Jodi smiled.

"Hmm, not sure about that," said Quinn. "But I don't think it's real complicated; just because I don't take any shit doesn't mean I'm not happy. If I didn't stand up, I'd be selling out. I can't do that."

She said, "You're putting a lot on your shoulders, don't you think?"

Quinn nodded and smiled. "Well, I'd be disrespecting my father, who taught me not to take any shit."

"So you're writing a book?" she asked.

"How did you know about that?" Quinn said.

"I have a friend who teaches at Merritt Island...a former student of yours."

Quinn smiled. "You have friends?"

"Ha ha."

"Well, you do spend a lot of time talking to an old curmudgeon on this bench," he said.

"Maybe, I'll stop," Jodi answered, with false indignation.

"Oh don't do that," Quinn said seriously. "You're a breath of fresh air."

"Why, Mr. Quinn..."

––––––––––––

Jodi read from a slip of yellow paper then handed it to Quinn: *Every new adjustment is a crisis in self esteem*

"Eric Hoffer," he said.

She smiled and said, "Yeah, I thought of you when I found it."

Quinn held on to the slip of paper for a moment, gently rubbing it with his thumbs. "So you think I oppose school reforms for the wrong reason?"

"I think maybe you're feeling insulted because you're being told to change," she said.

"Oh, I'm being insulted alright," Quinn answered, nodding his head. "Make no mistake about that." He paused. "Are you setting me up?

"What do you mean?" she asked.

"Don't trip my trigger on this, Jodi," he cautioned. "I'll go off on some crazy diatribe about the denaturing of teaching. You don't want to hear it."

"Denaturing?" Jodi asked, "Something about that word doesn't sound right."

Quinn bit into an apple.

"*Denature*," she read from her phone, "to take away or alter the natural qualities of."

He smiled. "Look up *deadfall*."

"A tangled mass of fallen trees and brush."

"How bout *identikit*?" he asked.

"Pardon me?" Jodi checked.

"I'll save you the time. Identikit teaching. That's what they want." Quinn made quotation marks in the air. "Created by putting together many different features that we have in common with little or no individual character."

"I don't follow," she said.

"Common Core," Quinn continued. "Cookie-cutter reforms resulting in the creation of all things unremarkable. Unexceptional people, ideas, things…teachers and students exactly the same as all of the others and not the least bit original."

Jodie squirmed. "You don't think teachers can be original anymore?

"Under these policies?" Quinn began to slap that back of his left hand in the palm of his right. "Every facet of authenticity is under attack," Quinn ranted. "To maintain any sense of individualism, you have to break the rules; and the kids don't know what to make of you. They think you're a nut because you're different."

She crossed her arms.

"Look, I've taught some sharp kids," Quinn said. "Bright, individualistic, free-thinking…some of them were sons and daughters of my bosses! How can students thrive in such an environment? And how in the hell can kids who aren't as bright and curious develop in that atmosphere?"

"That's not the intent, Quinn."

"Yeah, it may not be the intent but that's certainly the result. Educators and administrators endorse teaching methods and standards that address the 3% who are incompetent. Whether it's intentional or not," Quinn raved on, "the result is these requirements are sucking the rest of us dry. We spend hours covering our asses." Quinn noticed his voice getting really loud. "We're even coached on using the right catch phrases in our self-assessments and professional growth plans. That's not collaboration to me…that's…"

"So, where do we go from here?" asked Jodi.

Quinn finally caught himself and smiled. "Sorry for the rant."

"No, where do we go from here?" she said again.

"We're not talking about dogs on the beach."

"I have no idea what that means," Jodi said.

"Well, I'm afraid that we've created, or are in the midst of creating a teaching counter-culture. Administrators know there is active resistance, and it's often too much trouble to stop, but that will only last as long as tenure does. And Jodi," said Quinn with resignation, "that won't be around for long."

"So?"

"So, identikit."

"Oh my," she said. "I think I need a drink." Jodi took a long tug off her water bottle. "So what changed?" "How did we get here?"

"The Hot Lunch Program," Quinn answered quickly.

"Pardon?"

Quinn went into history teacher mode. "During the Depression, FDR's administration thought every kid should get a nourishing meal, since there was a good chance they weren't getting it at home."

"Sounds like a good idea," Jodi said.

"Yeah, it was," he continued, "but it didn't stop at lunch. Remember, this is public education, driven by politics. Steadily, public schools have become the surrogate parent. Anything perceived as lacking in the home became the responsibility of teachers. Hot Lunch culture. *Today, class, we'll start off with a nice warm bowl of self-esteem, and later on, we'll have some civility and manners.*"

"You bring sarcasm to a new level."

"Thank you."

"It's always been like this," Jodi said. "We've always been struggling to do our jobs in the face of every social problem that faces society. Violence, drugs, poverty, bad parenting; no parenting…"

"You're right," said Quinn. "The problem is public education has evolved into this institution—this conduit—through which government believes it can fix any domestic issue that rears its head. By assuming that role, it takes on actual education problems with the same approach. Common Core initiatives cut through the system like chemotherapy, taking the good with the bad."

"Tough analogy, Quinn," Jodi said, cringing.

"Yeah. And beware of the high priests if you question their dogma," Quinn said.

"Oh, I get it, you're an infidel."

...from the ghost
of Woody Guthrie
Education Reform in the hands of reckless idealists...

"And the wind shifts
And the dust on the doorsill shifts
And even the writing of the rat footprints
Tell us nothing, nothing at all
About the greatest city, the greatest nation, Where the
strong men listened
And the women warbled: nothing like us ever was."
-Carl Sandburg

Can you imagine a school with some of the best math and science teachers in the region working alongside commercial art and graphic design instructors; right next to journalism, drama, culinary arts, and building trades teachers? What would it be like to have auto mechanics and electronics classes so good that people in the community brought their cars and appliances to school for students to repair?

Before we write all this off as a pipedream, let's remember that much of what I just described was the Melbourne High School of the 1960's and 70's. Did I mention the silk screening class that printed all of the T-shirts and uniforms for the clubs and teams? How about the drafting students who walked right into salaried jobs at Harris Corporation? Mechanics and electricians jumped right into the workforce after graduation.

When I came out of school still thinking I was going to play centerfield for the rest of my life, a narrow curriculum was not to blame. I had been exposed to a plethora of vocational and avocational opportunies.

If we are to fix America's education problems, it's going to require us to look both forward and backward. It must be as President Reagan said, "Morning in America, again." We need to raise our expectations.

Let's send spending on education through the roof. Spend so much damn money that it corrupts our children! Build a school system so wondrous that it convinces them that knowledge is truly sacred. Construct schools that raise students' expectations of learning— schools that inspire awe when one walks down the halls.

How do we pay for it? How do we pay for the wars? How do we pay for anything? Frederick Douglass said we can't have crops without plowing the ground. Fiscal responsibility can only begin with a value system, and education must be **our first priority**. How can it not be at the top of our list?

Let's spoil our youth by creating schools burgeoning with every conceivable educational luxury...spoil them rotten! Make sparks fly around their heads! Raise teachers' salaries to an embarrassingly high level—so high that the profession begins to attract the best and brightest of each community! Make it so the young and creative minds are battling for the opportunity to teach. Free them from a bureaucracy that strangles spontaneous engagement with students.

Build entrances to schools that drop the jaws of all who walk through. Establish a reverence for learning from the first step. Place inscriptions of Dante` and Cicero above the doorways. Build classrooms with high ceilings and tile floors, so the words of wisdom echo off the walls. The majesty of the rooms themselves would command young men to take off their hats upon entering.

Construct libraries three stories tall—cathedrals to antiquity— with oak stairways and balconies. Place busts of Shakespeare, Frost, Hemingway, and Lincoln to gaze down upon the students. Plant ivy on the outside walls and build a commons area that would make Jefferson proud. Make buildings worthy of housing the works of Emily Dickinson and the passion of Martin Luther King.

Build auditoriums with architecture that celebrates the performing arts, and make athletic facilities that invite a commitment to excellence from each and every soul who competes.

Create science labs that unleash the curiosity of young minds. Bring back drawing and sculpture classes, auto mechanics, and masonry.

Bury standardized achievement tests. Bury them deep. Then set those teachers free to teach with reckless abandon. Walk away from a system that nurtures mediocrity and protects weakness and incompetence. Address the needs of the 97% who are good teachers and stop making blanket policies targeting the 3% who are not.

Allocate so much to schools that the gadflies scream, "BOONDOGGLE!" Create a public outcry for **doing too much**! Shake the windows and rattle the walls. Pour those tax dollars into the system! Take solace in doing the right thing. Look to the morning.

Then we can sit back and listen to some who will tell us we've spent too much on our youth; we've invested too much in our future; we've squandered too much to preserve our heritage. Is there such a thing as too much?

Free Ranging

...an American Education

Fareed Zakharia wrote an important book recently. It was called *In Defense of a Liberal Education.* When that word pops up we get all nervous, even the liberals themselves. Politicians stole the word. We're stealing it back. *Liberal* has no partisan meaning; no ideology. Like so many terms, it's been hijacked. Its meaning has been twisted and turned to accommodate belief systems. China and Iran call themselves *republics;* North Korea describes itself as the *Democratic People's Republic,* for crying out loud. Americans either run from the stigma linked to the word *liberal,* or use it as a club to beat opponents over the head. Enough.

Liberal derives from the Latin, *liberalis,* which is defined in the Oxford Dictionary as "relating to a free man." As I've said over and over, it all begins with unfettered freedom. The individual is bound only, in Jefferson's words, "by moderate powers of his own choice." In discussing education, liberal is an indispensible term, and Zakaria correctly identified a liberal education as an essential part of our culture. To roam freely through an open range of subjects allows the individual to try to make sense of the world.

Free ranging is what I like to call it. It's not just grazing, it's a rigorous but boundless pursuit of knowledge and skills, which give a person the means to engage responsibly in the world. By pursuing a broad range of subjects and letting one's interest and passion lead him, Zakaria claimed that the individual is much more prepared for the future than by simply learning vocational or career skills. A liberal education doesn't just teach a student computer skills, it also teaches her the physics which made the computer possible.[59]

---

[59]Fareed Zakaria, *In Defense of a Liberal Education* (New York: W.W. Norton & Company Ltd., 2015)

From time to time I come across a student who is frustrated with his math class. For encouragement, I remind him that the simple exercise of learning math is making him smarter.

By focusing on building broader strengths — reading; writing; historical knowledge; scientific understanding — we establish foundational ideas...we teach students to think for themselves. I can't help but remember my mentor's words: *Our job is not to teach them what to think, but how to think.*

Remembrance

Remembrance.
Laundered recollections.
Tearful goodbyes.
Vain but noble tries
To give a glimpse or glance
Behind his frail disguise.

What had to be said
Was said;
Necessary but inadequate
Thought Lincoln.
Words destined to miss their mark.

A piece of the past about
To be placed upon the shelf
He, the departed, had been
To a few of these himself—
Never caring for priest or preacher
Using the occasion…this heavy day
To reach out to the stray.
"Walk away from death,"
The old cowboy had warned.
"Walk away."

All he hoped for were bagpipes.
Bagpipes and a few funny stories.
But he got the 23rd Psalm
And a 400 year old hymn
Written by a slave ship captain
In a hurricane.

And then the wretched silence,
Broken only by coughs and sobs
And the clearing of throats.

A palpable restlessness...
Collective thoughts
Of wanting to be somewhere else--Anywhere else.

"Walk away from it," we heard
The cowboy say again.
But then, suddenly, music.
What's this?
Saxophone...Violin...acoustic guitar?

A sharp beat of drums,
Then a cannabis-worn voice.
Without a doubt, his own choice
To salve our souls;
Harkening a better, brighter day.

Two girls in sundresses,
Barefoot;
Slide out of their pew
And start dancing
In the aisle.

Ain't it funny how music takes on a life of its own?
Strange how it move us — how rhythm gets its way.

A man in a blue suit — arms folded
Seems annoyed at the irreverence
But soon finds his own foot tapping.

A young man wearing a borrowed tie, is up
And he dances like he doesn't care

Music seems to grow louder somehow
And two or three more have made their way
To the front,
And his daughter's up
And she's got her shoes off
And they are all dancing.

April 14

Quinn sat at his desk listening to the rain hit the roof. He sipped his coffee, trying to remember his password...

Email:

8:15 Jodi: No bench time today...I was looking forward to it...you got me thinking...

8:20 Quinn: Good Morning...it's a soft day in Ireland

9:48 Jodi: So I'm sitting in my Lit class, listening to the kids as they... work on their projects, avoid working on their projects, attempt to work on their projects but instead get sidetracked by all the stuff that consumes them: plans for an upcoming trip to Cancun; a discussion of whether or not gender is an assumed/assigned identity; inquiries into my tattoo. (It's a mullet, by the way. Straight from my copy of the FWC handbook. They just can't wrap their heads around my choice, no matter HOW many times they bring it up.)

10:10 Quinn: Neither can I (smiling)

10:12 Jodi: What's the parenthetical smiling mean? Not into emoticons?

11:25 Quinn: Not really

11:30 Jodi: Not sure how to explain my thoughts, but you got me thinking the other day...so you're going to just get some random stuff. Bear with me...(I have to eat something)

1:03 Jodi: Still raining...you know Quinn, I know everyone's bitching about teaching nowadays... and I agree, some of the changes have just plain sucked. I miss my second planning period. I cringe at the idea of submitting lesson plans, I get over our admin's idealistic but absolutely unrealistic proposals. Some of the changes piss me off because they inconvenience me, or don't seem to recognize how busy I already am, but others I just resent because I don't think they're actually going to improve my teaching or my students' learning. BUT, even though I can rant along with the best of them, the honest truth is, I still love my job. I am in it for the long-term. I love making the kids laugh; I love relating to them; I love hearing that Mr. Darcy is a badass; that they had to put *The Kite Runner* down for a few days because it was too intense; that they hate Edna Pontellier so vehemently that they CAN'T hold on til the class discussion starts to tell me about it, damnit! I love having an audience, to be honest, and I love that they keep me young. I love seeing the kids in the grocery store, chatting with their moms and dads at Longdogger's, catching up with them when they sneak back on campus that first spring break after they graduate. Even, God help me, lesson planning. I relish the idea of sitting back over the summer and reflecting and making plans for what novels we will delve into in the fall, how I'll connect the various texts and themes with my underclassmen. I don't want to be forced to put my ideas into any given template, or to submit it to a higher-up, but I love reflecting on what went well and what could have been better... I love the idea of reinventing myself and improving my craft when August rolls around. That's something I love about teaching: in what other career you get a defined start and finish line, where you get to step back and assess and start over every ten months? It's just awesome.

1:23 Quinn: Whew!

1:25 Jodi: Yeah, I love it...and I don't want to lose this...any of it. I'm afraid that I will.

1:30 Quinn: You don't seem to me to be afraid of much of anything.

3:27 Jodi: Dr.'s appointment tomorrow. Maybe I'll see you Thursday (smiling)

3:40 Quinn: That would be good.

Friends and Mentors

You know, as we grow older, we gain the understanding of how others have impacted our careers--our lives. Through the early years of teaching at Melbourne High School, I was surrounded by people who led me, guided me, inspired me and even scolded me. And in the case of Lloyd Soughers and Don Beggs, who both had a hand in hiring me (and not firing me), I am especially grateful. So here we are. As the years roll on, I've realized that I've been blessed not only by those who have blazed a trail before me, but by those who have fought the fight alongside me.

Years ago, a fellow teacher must have gotten wind that I was butchering a few poems in front of my history classes…probably limericks or song lyrics. That Christmas, I found a book of poetry in my mailbox. I was truly honored to receive a gift from someone I so admired and respected. The book changed the way I taught, and most certainly changed the way I thought. Thank you, Ms. Joanne Steady.

Joanne was an English teacher who was always after more than producing dependable employees — students adept at something more than an eloquent reading of the menu at Denny's. My colleague shared a common conviction that education is more than training young people for occupational placement.

I treasure those copy-room conversations when she would get caught up in describing the writing of one of our students as "wonderful…powerful!" I could hear the absolute joy in her voice. Now, there were times…when I could hear other things in her voice, when she was venting! Sometimes, success is, as Churchill once said, simply moving amongst our failures without losing enthusiasm.

In appreciating the English teacher's work, we need to try to grasp the special significance of her job. Language allows us not only to communicate with others, but also with ourselves. And to learn this language is empowering beyond measure. As long as I've known her, Joanne has carried this burden of responsibility with integrity and grace and dogged determination

Our days as teachers are often jammed with the the tasks of administrative accountability. And adding to that, everywhere we turn, there seems to be something negative going on within our profession. But even in the wake of frustration and exhaustion, Mr. Jim Lewis taught me, by example, to search for those rare but pure specks of creativity and curiosity—the diamonds in the dust.

Jim Lewis, also an English teacher, was a renaissance man. By the time we met, he had done more in his life than I had even read about in mine. Jim brought with those experiences an intellectual presence, the likes of which I have not encountered before or since. There was a gentleness to his character, a humility; that was strangely incongruent with his rough-hewn life experiences. Jim was a cowboy and a Vietnam War veteran. But he was also a poet and an accomplished ballroom dancer. He was the sort of guy that you knew was in the room before you saw him. Through all of this, it was Jim Lewis who volunteered to take on a class filled with troubled borderline seniors who were in danger of not graduating. His view: *everybody needs some Shakespeare, not just Honors students.* Not surprisingly, Jim thrived under those circumstances, and so did his students. By the end of the year, those kids were reciting poetry in front of the class. Yes, teaching is a struggle—no doubt it's always been this way…so be it. If you fight the fight with but a fraction of the integrity of Joanne Steady and Jim Lewis, it becomes a noble struggle.

We work within a new evaluation system which places a big emphasis on collaboration, but let me tell you, it was already a subtle yet powerful force in this profession. More spontaneous in form, collaboration has always been an integral part of the teaching community. And I'm guilty of taking much more than I've ever given back.

I attended a meeting a while back and listened to collaborative ideas from my colleagues It's safe to say I didn't have much to share with them, but man, I walked away feeling good about teaching and teachers. My batteries were recharged—and that usually requires something served at the local pub. In one case, I saw a teacher still giving a fresh perspective after decades in the classroom. And in offering up her ideas, she was offering up herself—and thus revealing maybe her greatest strength—authenticity. I'm thinking that that may well be the most important component of teaching. We deal with a pretty tough audience everyday...and they can see through us in a heartbeat. One of the highest duties of a teacher...of a human for that matter — is to remain true to herself and let the chips fall where they may.

Collaboration's a pretty easy concept. A teacher must learn in order to teach, so we must be forever the students. There seems to be very little light between our own teachers, our gifted colleagues, and our students. We learn from all of them.

I'm not sure where Bill Carey fits in all this. Friend? Mentor? Hero? There's seldom a time when Bill isn't the smartest guy in the room. He was a great Math teacher, athletic director, coach, and counselor. He took me under his wing when I was a 24 year old raging jackass and taught me what I needed to know in order to thrive in the profession. Scores of young teachers owe a debt of gratitude to William Barry Carey. He became an adopted Irish uncle whom I never wanted to disappoint. Whether we were sitting in the bleachers at a Spring Training ballgame or on a barstool in Savannah, Bill offered sage advice. He taught me how to forge relationships with students, and I realized early on that the trust I built with them only bolstered my efforts to inspire a love for knowledge. I learned from Bill to choose my battles; to keep my sense of humor close; and to never sell out...never. He's a stubborn man, and stubbornness can be an indispensible quality in this profession.

Bill's influence is still being felt years after he retired to grandfatherhood. He's a mountain of a man and as our friend Nick Wright once said, "Bill Carey's footprints might not be the biggest, but they're certainly the deepest." Greg Skufca and Wayne Cattell were two of Bill's protégés in the Math department. Greg was a great teacher and any student who passed through his classroom door will attest to the fact that Wayne Cattell was one of the best teachers they've encountered. Wayne is an AP Calculus teacher. The closest I ever came to that course was dating a girl who took Calculus.

Maybe my favorite thing about Wayne Cattell doesn't involve his tireless efforts in the classroom, but his relentless efforts to become a good teacher. Wayne spent his early years becoming knowledgeable and effective — learning his song, so to speak. Not only did he practice, he pumped his colleagues dry for help. He would literally beg his fellow math teachers to help him with a problem. I've seen him do it. This requires both a great deal of determination and humility. Nothing was more important to Wayne than learning his craft. Of course, he's now at the top of his game, and Wayne is the one helping the young teachers learn. Anyone who knows him knows that he loves cowboys and cowboy movies. I always quote his favorite movie to him, making light of his work ethic: "You do more than your share of the work, so I keep the balance by doing less." That's not exactly true, but I do love to pull his chain.

There have been many times in my career when I could feel fatigue setting in—when I felt worn down by this wonderful yet burdensome job. But I kept on grinding; because I knew that somewhere on the campus, Wayne Cattell and Joanne Steady and Donna Donovan were pushing onward. And I felt that if I relented—if I gave in—I would be somehow doing them a disservice. So, in always asking more of themselves, it required— it demanded—that those around them ask more of ourselves.

When it comes right down to it, a history teacher is a story-teller; what the Irish call a shanachie: a bearer of old lore; teller of tales; spinner of yarns.

Many of the finest teachers I know are good story-tellers. Without question, the finest one around is my friend and colleague, Pete Donovan. His stories are hilarious without exception. I still sneak into the back of his room just to listen to one I know I've heard at least a dozen times. Students are so riveted to his lesson, they don't even realize they're learning.

Pete possesses the best instincts of any teacher I've known. Even after three decades in the classroom, there is something about his teaching that I can't quite put my finger on...something unique and spontaneous. It comes from the gut. Pete instinctively knows what works and he'd be annoyed at me for trying to analyze it. He's very self-effacing concerning his skills as a teacher and baseball coach, but don't let him fool you; he's confident and committed to what he does. We started teaching together and now we're both growing old. Pete tries to come off as this grumpy curmudgeon, but it doesn't fly. His students and players see right through him.

A few years back, Pete had a senior whose family moved out of the district during her final semester. Because of the move, she no longer had access to bus transportation. She was missing her morning classes on a regular basis and was in danger of not graduating. Pete Donovan gave her money out his own pocket so she could ride the city transit to school for the last two months. She graduated. Not many people know about that. Pete's often guilty of doing a good thing when no one is looking.

I've always told my share of tales, and Pete convinced me through the years that maybe it all comes down to stories. Don't get me wrong, we history teachers (and students) need to be good detectives. We must comb through the facts, the motives, and the plots with great care. But a figurative expression of truth can only fortify a literal expression of fact.

Unfortunately, in our efforts to be objective, we often sanitize history; making it into a harmless product. In order to keep it free – or appear to be free – of any political spin, we're often guilty of sucking the life out of the lesson. To be honest, our present evaluation system is a sham. It's an extensive, time-consuming, painstaking process in which teachers demonstrate to nonteachers that they are fulfilling numerous requirements in class. We spend more time talking and writing about collaboration that we do collaborating. Somewhere along the way, they changed the definition of accountability. Today, it means "cover your ass."

To be fair, *there are many exciting new ideas coming into teaching, but that doesn't mean that the old ways don't work.* As I said, Pete Donovan is one of the least pretentious people you'll meet. He failed the course on self-promotion. Because he refuses to jump through the hoops, he's often overlooked when it comes to getting the recognition he deserves. "Just leave me alone and let me teach," he'd say. When we try to dissect a lesson in a good teacher's class, we are often guilty of, as Frost said, rendering "ungraceful what he…had faith he had made graceful." We can very easily hunt it down and kill it. It's like trying to explain a joke to someone. If you don't get it, you don't get it.

I am reminded again of my old American History professor, Frank Merritt. Although this Tennessean was well into his sixties by the time I got to his class, he still made sparks fly around our heads. "Come early and stay late!" And he was true to his word; starting his lectures ten minutes early and then dragging them at least five minutes beyond the end.

Although Professor Merritt was not the most knowledgeable instructor I ever came across, he was without a doubt the most passionate. He was part Baptist preacher, part Shakespearean actor. I can still see him throwing himself around the room while reenacting Jackson's duel. I can still hear him hollering out of window, heralding the end of the Civil War. During the second course I took with him, I couldn't help but gaze around and find the first-timers so spellbound by the performance, they forgot to take notes!

When a student questioned the old professor about a date or a name, he wagged his finger, smiled and replied, "Don't let your facts get in the way of the truth, son." I think he was on to something.

Today's the Day

A message to my students

Good Morning...Hello...G'day...Great Day? The coffee tastes especially good today.

"Today's the day!" I once read that each morning Mel Fisher greeted everybody with that line. He may well have been speaking of his relentless search for Spanish treasure, but perhaps there was more on his mind.

He spent 16 years searching for the Atocha. Was it all easy? Was it all good? Hardly. Fisher fought off bankruptcy, scandal, personal tragedy, and the United States government. Nevertheless, he greeted everyone each morning with that great salutation: "Today's the Day!"

A life can be reduced to moments; experiences transitory in nature...fleeting...at the very instant we're experiencing them, they are already slipping through our fingers. To be sure, there are times we recognize as special, and instinctively try to capture the moment with videos and still pictures, only to miss it in the effort to hold on to it!

Now I've said so myself that there is happiness in the warm expectancy of finding something good in tomorrow, but the joy of anticipation can't rob me of discovering something good about today.

Everybody's talking about tomorrow. Tomorrow this and tomorrow that; as if our lives are set to begin on some future date. *When I get out of school...when I pay off my debts...when I move out on my own...***your life is now**.

I remember being young. I like to think there's a lot of young still in me. (don't spoil it by saying it ain't so). What's great about being young is the promise of many days ahead. We spend time like it was money we found in the parking lot. But there is a trap in our youth. By always looking forward and upward, we may overlook today and let *this day* slip away. Today is the day. The treasure is today.

My wish for you is a wealth of days, but not at the expense of the here and now. Louis L'Amour claimed that life can be divided into two parts: "anticipation and memory, and if we remember richly, we must have lived richly." Something today may well be the best thing; the funniest thing; the most beautiful thing; or maybe the saddest thing. It could be a thought; a phrase; a story; or maybe a person you encounter. Today...you might see or hear or read something that changes everything. Don't miss it.

We catch ourselves saying things like, "Get on with your life." I've given reassurances like "you've got plenty of time," when time is the least thing we have (Hemingway). "Where did all the time go?" we wonder. It's as if it was a hundred dollars we pissed away on Friday night...like it was other people's money. In retrospect, we say quaint little things like, "life got in the way." What in the hell does that mean anyway?

Well, we don't have other people's time. Only our own. I'm easily angered when someone wastes mine. Now don't get me wrong; that doesn't mean we have a moral obligation to be forever busy. John Lennon said, "Time enjoyed wasting is not wasted."

When bad things happen, we say: "get through this" or "get to the other side of this." Surely the goal is to endure and survive, but "life" can't be put on hold while we fight our battles. The battles are parts of your life...the good the bad and the ugly. Even on my worst day, there is an enormous amount of good—kids and dogs; oaks and palms; and orange moons rising.   Today's the day.

> Several years ago, I had just settled into a fine October afternoon of watching college football, when my wife asked me to run to the grocery store for something she had forgotten. Of course I would. With the proper navigation, I could make the trip at halftime and be back before the first play of the second half. I hid my irritation (no easy task) at having one of my favorite activities interrupted.
>
> Well, things went like clockwork; the half ended and I jumped into my Jeep and zipped over to the nearest Publix. There was only one elderly gentleman in front of me in the checkout line,

but I noticed that things were not going smoothly for him. He apparently put too much in his cart for what he had in his wallet, and the young cashier was patiently helping him figure out what he could buy and what had to go back.

I kept my respectful distance; doing my best not to appear hurried, but hurried I was. The second half kickoff was coming and I was far away from my recliner. Finally, they were finished. "Seventeen twenty nine," the cashier said softly. The old man paid and slowly pushed his cart away. Not until I opened my wallet did I realize what I had done, or had failed to do. With two twenties resting comfortably in my billfold, I could have easily covered what the old man lacked. In my haste…in looking past this moment toward another, I had missed a chance to help someone. In my anticipation to get to another moment I had missed this one. It floored me. I trudged to the Jeep and drove back to my precious football game.

I spent months trying to right the scales. Surely someone would need help and I would be there for the rescue! One day while driving down I-95, I finally saw my chance. As I approached a car on the side of the road with its emergency flashers on, I saw a pregnant woman leaning on the car with her head bowed. This was my chance! I was going too fast to stop so I switched lanes, cut through the grass median, and made a dramatic (and illegal) U-turn. I then sped to the exit and headed back toward the woman in need. By the time I arrived, however, another motorist had already stopped to help. Sigh.

I had no idea then that like the old mariner, I would be condemned to tell this story over and over (Alas, my penance). But I'm not sure it's just about acts of kindness. It may also be about teaching me to keep my eyes open….about the importance of the here and now.

Still, we talk of *spending time. Spending the day. How'd you spend the day?* I'll tell you how I spent the day: I grabbed it by the friggin' throat! I squeezed every ounce out of it. I sat on the hearth with my dogs and sipped Maxwell House coffee…black. I took a ridiculously hot shower listening to Robert Nesta Marley. I got irritated in traffic for the nine hundred and ninety ninth time, only to be knocked off balance by the sunrise and a pretty girl riding a bicycle. I cheerfully walked right by my boss three minutes late to work. Are you getting the picture?

If this day is mean or sublime or hectic, I'm plowing on, because there is something good in today; something unique and particular, and I don't want to miss it. In the face of fear and uncertainty; frustration and sadness; tedium and worry; there is something that makes this day like no other. So I have to keep my head up and my eyes open.

You never know when moments arrives that reaches to the core and changes you forever.

April 16

"How did your doctor's appointment go? Quinn asked.

"It went," she said. Jodi had fielded that question about five times in the last half hour

"Here, read this." Jodi handed him an index card. "One of my friends sent me this."

Quinn read it out loud:

> *How lucky I am to be needed...How blessed am I to love teaching and motherhood so much that I'm constantly lovesick for one or the other. To have your hands full is a ludicrous blessing!*

"Blythe sent you this, didn't she?" he asked.

"How'd you know?"

"That's her," said Quinn. "She's something. Keep listening to her...you'll learn more than you will from this old coot."

"I'm gonna tape it to the corner of my computer screen, right next to my mantra," Jodi said cheerily.

"Your mantra? Does it have anything to do with a mullet?"

"I am seeking, I am striving, I am in it with all my heart," she proclaimed. "Cheesy...but at my essence, I am irredeemably cheesy, so it works."

"Harrison says it's better to be cheesy than to die a smart ass," added Quinn.

Jodi said she liked that..."better than the raven quote."

"Really?"

The beauty of the afternoon was distracting. Gazing upward, Quinn thought of an old Frost line: *Lord, I have loved your sky, be it said against or for me*...the sound of a plane taking off from MLB broke the quiet. Locals would joke about the lack of activity at the airport. There weren't many flights in and out on a daily basis, making the terminal a nice place for solitude. The scarcity of flights served as an assurance that their town still had a touch of smallness. It was a false assurance. Florida was exploding. So many places had changed beyond recognition.

"If you don't mind...me asking..." Quinn spoke slowly, "What kind of... support system... do you and that baby have?" There were spaces between Quinn and his words.

"I don't mind you asking, as long as it's for the right reason." Jodi didn't make eye contact.

After a moment, Quinn said, "I can't think of what a wrong reason would be...but..."

"This is it," Jodi interrupted. "She and I," placing her hand on her belly. "And I don't need a man if that's what you're implying."

Quinn showed no emotion. He thought hard about how to get out of this conversation. It was not going the way he had intended. "You already know it's a girl?"

"Oh it's going to be a girl. It has to be."

Quinn could smell no fear in this woman. She was going to raise this kid on her own and she could already envision what she and the baby would do; the songs she will sing to her; the way the nursery will look from her rocking chair.

Jodi turned toward Quinn. "The girls here are giving me a shower. We'll be good. I'm looking for a good rocker, though, if you hear of something."

"That's right in my wheelhouse," Quinn said, fighting off the awkwardness. "My wife has a thing for rocking chairs; how 'bout a slide rocker?"

Quinn stopped at Ichabod's Dockside on the way home, hoping his brother-in-law would be there, but no such luck. He sat at the corner of the bar and drank two Red Stripes in the short brown bottles. He gazed out at the boats and talked to no one. The windows were open and a light breeze moved through the place. He knew his dogs were waiting for him, so he paid his tab and went on home.

"Our dogs spend a lot of time waiting," Quinn said to himself. "I have to believe that they'll be waiting for us again."

Bringing History Home

"Let's get to know each other a little better. You come in and sit down, I talk, you listen, and write down what I say. Got it?" Usually, during the first week of class those words come out of my mouth at one point or another.

The first order of business is to establish a mindset for learning note-taking. As my mentor taught me, my first responsibility is to provide students with as much knowledge as possible and "have faith that they can use it to think for themselves." Teaching history may be more than simply supplying facts and dates, but it certainly isn't less.

A great benefit of learning our history is the discovery of our personal connection to it. History is the glue of our civilization — shared memories build community in both personal and public circles. It is not always the president or the general who teaches us important life lessons. Stories of our past reveal people from all walks of life who possessed definitive and virtuous character traits. Such conceptions of character not only help us understand our time and place, but they also teach us how to live a responsible, rewarding, and interesting life.

Years ago, a new and different evaluation approach required teachers to come up with a project for students that would utilize different teaching strategies. To be honest, the priority was for teachers to demonstrate the use of methods other than lecture. Heaven forbid that we stick with something that has worked. Instead of fighting this one, I decided to jump through the hoop. In what appeared to be a recycled idea from elementary school, I came up with *Bringing History Home*. It became much more than that.

ASSIGNMENT: INTERVIEW A FAMILY MEMBER OR FRIEND TWO GENERATIONS REMOVED. USE THE FOLLOWING FORMAT AS THE BASIS FOR YOUR INTERVIEW.

- **BRIEF BIOGRAPHY:** *(1 OR 2 PARAGRAPHS)*
- **QUESTIONS:**

1. What is the one historical event in your life that you most vividly remember? Details? How did it affect you?
2. What historical figure possesses character traits you most admire and respect? Explain
3. **Above all others in your lifetime, what person has been the most influential? Explain**
4. Was there a time in your life when you felt particularly close to your community? Explain
5. What historical event do you consider to be the greatest in American History?
6. What event do you consider to be the worst in American History?
7. **Is there a story or a quote that best explains your sense of connection to the past?**

I urged the students to give their interviewee time to chew upon the questions, so they would get good reflective answers

Some students have already made connections with stories of their grandparents' and parents' generations, but most have not. Many are disconnected or estranged from family members in a way that makes this a very tough task. Some families are so separated from their past that it becomes a tedious exercise for the student to awaken the memories of her family members. But for others, the stories flow. For some, the memories are so thick, as they say, they have to brush them away from their faces.

I sometimes give a student the option to interview a neighbor or an older person with whom they come in contact, but most of the time I hold them to the fire. They must realize how World War II takes on a different meaning when they find out a great grandfather fought in it; or The Great Depression carries a greater significance when the discover their grandparents survived it.

Now I'm not going to tell you that this assignment breaks down the barriers of communication in each family, and that it gives us 27 epiphanies a year. Many students get out if it exactly what they put into it. Unfortunately, some try their level best and get nothing.

But when it works, it works! Christopher Hitchens said an effective teacher must remain a student, and these project keep me learning from my kids. Annie's Belgium story about her grandparents being caught literally in the middle of World War II gave me insight I never possessed. Tatiyana's gripping tale of how her grandfather stayed alive in the concentration camps knocked me out of my chair.

Several weeks after we complete the first project, students get the second:

ASSIGNMENT 2:

A. Ask three people to answer the following questions:
- A grandparent
- A parent, aunt or uncle
- A sibling or friend

 1. *What are the most admirable traits in a person?*

 2. **How would you define a "successful" life?**

B. Identify 5 people who possess what you would consider to be virtuous or admirable traits.

C. Identify 5 people of the past or present who have lived successful lives.

D. Are Lists B and C the same? How and Why do they
    differ?

Where do these projects fit in our History lessons? In one way
or another, all history is personal, and projects like   these may
allow a student to experience a sense of interconnectedness,
maybe for the first time.

How does it feel to suffer from migraines? …to get shot at?
…to battle depression? What's it like to be homeless? …to leave
your family and friends to fight for people you don't even know?
How does it feel to be arrested? …to know in your heart that
you're right when everybody's saying you're wrong? …or how
does it feel to believe in something for a long time only to discover
you're dead wrong?

Behold, the doctrine of unintended outcomes! If students can
stumble upon stories of family struggles, perhaps they can better
understand George Washington's circumstances. Or Lincoln's.
Can they fully realize what it was like at Normandy? Or
Gettysburg? Or Valley Forge? Can they comprehend the
humiliation of losing one's home during the Depression? Can they
appreciate the courage it took for Rosa Parks to sit down on the
bus; or for Jefferson to write the Declaration even in the midst of
great personal tragedy…even in the face of his own hypocrisy?

Compared to some other strategies we use, this one is sort of
inside out. Instead of using great and famous characters to help
inspire us in our personal lives, *Bringing History Home* can
hopefully use the personal to better comprehend the prolific. This
is where heroes come in.

Tropical Shirts

Shelby Strother was a Florida boy
Whose talents took him far and wide;
Across the great divide and back again.
From Denver to Detroit, this writer he did roam,
But he could not hide
His love and pride for home.

And though we never really met,
He's a man I never can forget;
Whose stories they grow dearer yet
As I grow even older.

No matter where he went—how far he was away,
He wore those tropic prints
Until his dying day.
And lest the memory grows dim,
I've worn them often ever since
As a way to honor him.

Someone asked me once about them—
Some are gaudy; some are loud;
A few are frayed around the collar
And the sleeves;
I wear them proud.
Perhaps there is a hint of what this fool believes,
But don't judge a book by its shirt.

Shelby wrote of his days living
On the Earth—what he saw and what he heard.
Each link in chain, he worked the words--
The perfect and the non—
There is a difference.

We may be blinded to the goings-on
By blazing sun and stinging rains;
And it's so hard at times
To see the love and beauty
In the relics and remains.

Time like a river races by, it's been said
But there are words that capture time
…and keep it still…briefly.
As still as a Florida summer morning.

From transitory moments
There are mysteries revealed,
In fleeting commonplace events
On courts and playing fields.
For Shelby, there was always something.

Conversations at fish camps and boat ramps.
Of baseball and basketball
And knocking down the Berlin Wall;
 Of Dad and Mom
And Vietnam.
…a painted dawn and stories of old Honest John;
Biographs and Epitaphs,
A Cracker Woman who shook all over
When she laughed.
…shook all over when she laughed.

And so I wear the shirts
As often as I can
To remember — to remind me of a man
With soul —
What the jazzman said makes other folks
Feel better about being alive.

April 21

"Did you ever walk down River Street in Savannah at night...or maybe downtown Asheville, and listen to the street musicians?" Quinn asked.

"Austin's the place," Jodi added, "I hear Nashville is something else."

"Then you know what I mean," said Quinn. "You stroll along and stop to hear those you feel are worth listening to. There was this sax player down by the water in Savannah who captivated me...he wouldn't let me take his picture, though. I always thought teaching, at its best, offered students an intellectual stroll."

"Hmm," Jodi said, as she brushed her hair away from her face. "Never thought of it that way."

"Those, my dear, are some of the best words in the language. *I never thought of it that way.* I like to call it *free ranging*...to roam freely through an open range of subjects, letting your interests and passions lead you," Quinn explained.

"*Free ranging,*" Jodi repeated, chewing on the words. "Reminds me of a Robert Duvall-Tommy Lee Jones movie."

"Exactly."

"What? Education is like driving cattle to Montana?" Jodi asked.

"No," Quinn said. "but it is about sitting around the campfire reading Leviticus, waiting for the biscuits to be done. And it is about barroom conversations among Texas Rangers...and Key West fishermen."

After a moment of quiet, Quinn went on. Jodi was getting used to the pauses. "Jodi, I read an interesting book a while back by Fareed Zakaria. It's called *In Defense of a Liberal Education.*"

"There's that word everybody's scared of...'liberal'..."

"Politicians stole that word," Quinn said. "We're stealing it back."

"So, what about the book?" she asked.

"Zakaria said that a liberal education is a fundamental part of American culture. A rigorous but boundless pursuit of knowledge — *free ranging*." Quinn was talking with his hands.

"Quinn, do you know how much energy I spend trying to get kids excited about reading?" Jodi asked rhetorically. "I reach maybe a handful."

"Oh, I think you're doing much more than you think, Jodi," " he assured.

"Yeah, most of them think it's a waste of time," she said. "The only reason they're here — the only purpose of education is to prepare them for a job...or get them to college to prepare them for a job."

"That's dead wrong," Quinn said. "And I think a liberal education better prepares them for a career, anyway."

"It's a grind," she said with a sigh in her voice. Quinn had never heard her sound so low.

"Oh yeah, it's a grind, but a noble one!" "Remember," he said, "we're not tanks or bulldozers, we're screwdrivers...that's Jim Harrison, by the way."

Jodi took a drink from her water bottle.

Quinn stopped. After a long silence, he broke it. "No moon this morning."

She said nothing.

"Spring mornings are glorious. First light, clear sky, but there was no moon this morning. I think it set before the sun did yesterday. Waning crescent, I believe. A fingernail moon."

"Where are you going with this?"

"Jodi, there are moments wrapped up in the struggles and the strife. This job, like everything else, comes down to pieces and parts — slices and flashes — whether they be great victories, tests of character, or simple experiences in the daily routine. And to thrive, you gotta see the world as Proust said, with new eyes."

Jodi stared straight ahead.

Quinn was pretty sure he wasn't reaching her. She seemed a few miles away. "Love among the ruins, Jodi," he said.

She sat back and looked at him.

"There are specks of creativity and curiosity in the dust — there in the dust. And sometimes you gotta squint. Harrison says you gotta squint."

"There's Harrison again." Jodi shook her head and smiled. Wherever she had gone, she seemed to be back. "Tell me more about *free ranging*, Mr. Quinn."

Quinn wasn't so sure he wanted to drag her through his spiel. "Didn't mean to preach."

"Yes you did."

He laughed. "Ah, it's just we have to fortify ourselves — build up our resistance to whatever those pudknocker educators are trying to sell us."

"So…"

"We need to change their mindset, Jodi, one student at a time. If we can get them to ask different questions, that would be a big step. Instead of walking in asking, *what do I have to do to get the grade in this class?* We have to get them asking, *what can I learn about the world today?...or what can I learn that could possibly change my life today?*"

Jodi said, "You may be as cheesy as I am. I should be taking notes."

"Well, I am writing a book," Quinn said. Then they both laughed.

"My object in living is to unite my vocation with my avocation as my two eyes make one in sight."

"What's that from…Frost?" she asked.

Two Tramps at Mudtime. One of my favorites," he said.

"I have a few friends working in the business world," Jodi said. "Finance majors…marketing…computers. They say most of the stuff they learned in college is totally useless when it comes to their jobs."

"Amen. My son learned that first hand," Quinn answered. "Anything you need you can pick up in a few months, and besides, things vary from job to job."

"So…?" Jodi kicked off her shoes.

"Teach them to think for themselves. Focus on building broader strengths, as Zakaria said. Teach 'em to write; to read; give them some historical knowledge and some basic scientific understanding…foundational ideas!"

Jodi was ready with her question: "Quinn, how do you get them to love learning?"

"Hell, Jodi, you know as much as I do on that one. I guess it starts with loving it yourself. Whether it's the story or just the pure act of teaching (grammar…dead presidents…what have you), you have to be attached to it for a lesson to have any real meaning. Only when the lesson is delivered within a story or a circumstance can it be absorbed into a students' understanding. I believe that."

Quinn went on. "I used to tell my ballplayers that they needed a little bit of 'I don't give a damn' to be good, and I think that's also true of teaching. There are times when motivational techniques become counterproductive."

"I'm not sure I follow," said Jodi.

"Splendid Indifference. Here." Quinn handed her a manila folder.

Splendid Indifference

My high school English teacher once stood in front of my class and read *Beowulf* out loud...in Old English. My 17-year-old mind couldn't help but think it bizarre, but part of me felt stirred by the whole experience. Here she was, expecting a bunch of adolescents to appreciate the beauty of the language. Her love for the story blinded her to the shallow cynicism of her audience. It was as if she didn't give a damn whether we liked it all. This was not necessarily just about *Beowulf*, and when I realized that, it struck me.

She seemed unable to hide her own love for the words. She would not push them on us; nor try to sell us on their value. Try as she did, though, she couldn't keep the treasure to herself. As naïve as it may have seemed at the time, her splendid indifference actually opened the door much wider. We were being allowed a glimpse of enlightenment.

Perhaps I wasn't ready to turn away from the silhouettes on the wall and look directly at the light, but my teacher was letting me know that there was much more out there than shadows. I never got around to telling Ms. Grames. Or thanking her.

A teacher must possess the audacity to believe that students will naturally be interested in what he has to say. He can't internalize as failure the hard fact that he can't reach them all. You can't reach every student every day. Kids have a thousand things going, and there are times when they are going to be unexcited, unimpressed, uninspired, and uncurious.

Teachers have got to keep bits of that splendid indifference and let passion do its work. It's essential to teaching. As Bob Dylan proved years ago, there are times when you must let the audience come to you, rather than the other way around. Inspire the love of knowledge by loving it yourself. And they will come.

Biograph

(so far)

He dove down into the clear green water of the Atlantic; he read the Declaration of Independence…studied it; made fires in all kinds of weather; dodged a waterspout in the Gulf… jumped off a railroad bridge into the Peace River; drank Mexican beer. He played centerfield; fell off a roof, had a job digging ditches. Sang songs to his children as they fell asleep; burned some bridges; slid down a North Carolina rock into freezing water; broke some rules…stumbled while watching a beautiful girl pass by…smoked a Cuban cigar. Ruined friendships over pride…saved some friendships by swallowing his pride. Got born and raised in Florida…Melbourne, Florida; saw dolphins jump not twenty feet from the bow of his boat…he read the Bill of Rights as often as he could; kept some secrets; played his music too loud.

He once cursed and prayed in the same sentence. He loved books…liked the way books smelled—old and new…loved baseball. He got seasick occasionally; nearly broke his ankle jumping into shallow water near Shell Island. Played catch with his son; he passed down stories of the great Ted Williams; let his ego get in the way; tried to listen to advice, didn't always follow it. Felt guilty, at times for good reason; other times, for no good reason. He pretended not to see someone he knew… got his feelings hurt when someone he knew pretended not to see him. Loved his wife and kids and dogs. Dove down into the coke bottle green water of the Gulf of Mexico; stayed awake all night; read Robert Frost to his children; fell asleep at the wheel. Got upset at a priest for his homily…took walks alone on the beach…went to Monticello; sat upon a surfboard out beyond the break and listened to the silence…read his favorite books over and over again…spent a lot of time in the Keys.

…went to a John Mellencamp concert; piloted his boat through a driving rain storm; got a speeding ticket while listening to John Mellencamp. Defended Marilyn Monroe's honor; felt the hair stand up on the back of his neck during The Star Spangled Banner;

saw Roberto Clemente play baseball...cultivated his Irish; took family walks along the beach...held his granddaughters, Savannah, Delaney, and Amelia.

...was known on occasion to scream at the television while watching political speeches; told the same stories over and over again; helped a few people...missed a lot of opportunities to help others. Watched the sunrise on the Sebastian Inlet jetty...took a swim in Brick Lake. He was by his father's side when he died...

He stood his ground when he should have given in; drank coffee from Café du Monde; tossed a quarter in the fish's mouth at Captain Tony's...he once met Captain Tony...had his picture taken with Captain Tony. Stopped going to Church after his mother died. Saw Pete Rose and George Brett play baseball; climbed a waterfall; he loved dogs...did I tell you he loved dogs? He read newspaper columns by Billy Cox; smoked a few cheap cigars...went back to Church after his kids were born.

Talked to neighbors; slept in a hammock one summer; avoided neighbors. Gave in when he should have stood his ground; cussed when he was angry...threw things when he was very angry; once bought a six-pack of beer with change. He loved the city of Savannah...pirated cobblestones from River Street in Savannah... Saw Carl Yastremski play left field...

Ran out of gas; read Thomas Paine's "Common Sense" several times; avoided phone-calls; picked up trash out of the river; watched "The Quiet Man" each and every St. Patrick's Day. Argued with umpires; talked to God; saw Willie Mays play baseball; loved the Pittsburgh Steelers. Steered his boat through 8 foot swells and wondered if he would see land again... talked too much...drank too much...didn't talk enough...at times, didn't drink enough.

tried to make eye contact as much as possible; cried at his daughter's dance recital... he spent numerous evenings waiting for a full moon to rise up out of the ocean...took his kids fishing; defended JFK's honor... gauged a man by his handshake.

…sat in the dark listening to Van Morrison; ate guava pie; studied the US Constitution; ripped the buttons off his shirt the night the Braves beat the Pirates for the pennant. Drank Guinness at Kevin Barry's in Savannah…let his dogs run on the beach…

He had his boat break down right in the middle of Sebastian Inlet…He read Jim Harrison; loved kids; quoted Thomas Jefferson and Bob Dylan in the same conversation; tried to have a firm handshake; bought his daughter a steel drum; got tears in his eyes the first time his son rode a bicycle. Took a 6-hour boat ride to Cabbage Key; ate fresh snapper fried light; once chopped down a tree onto the power lines; sat in the driving rain at a Florida-Georgia football game…liked to sit with friends around a bonfire.

…he talked often to his mother; listened to John Prine…admired Eugene V. Debs. Once went to Charleston, South Carolina by accident; wore tropical shirts as often as he could; he quoted his father daily. Hit a grand slam, built a Tiki bar, walked through graveyards in Connecticut, hitched a ride on a boat to get pizza. Read Louis L'Amour's "Mangrove Coast"…admired Martin Luther King, Jr…greatly admired Robert E. Lee.

…read James Dickey's "Rain Guitar" a hundred times but never memorized it; had a tire swing; made strange mobiles out of shells, driftwood, and crabtrap floats. He once had a job moving furniture; wrote letters to the editor of the local newspaper but seldom got them printed…had a Christmas in July party…once had two German Shepherds; drove a Jeep Wagoneer to the top of a mountain; played a ballgame while the KKK sat out beyond the left field fence.

Twice stood on the steps of the Lincoln Memorial — once with his kids…listened to Waylon Jennings…and Willie Nelson…and Kris Kristofferson…and Merle Haggard; prayed; fell for his wife on the Fourth of July.

He voted for Clinton Tyree for governor; saw just about every movie Robert Duvall ever made; read Carl Sandburg; built a swing off of the side of a North Carolina mountain…sang songs to his wife and kids (while they rolled their eyes). He liked to sit by himself around a bonfire.

Coached high school baseball; listened a lot to Bruce Springsteen…
owned a 1985 23-foot Mako. He liked to watch the phosphorescence
in the wake of a boat; was thrown out of a bar; wore out several
baseball caps—wore them out…lost touch with good friends…let his
son drive…he watched "Donovan's Reef" each Christmas. He knew
how to hook slide; collected license plates; had a Chocolate Lab
named Marley—before the book and movie, but after the prophet—
crazy dog, good friend. He loved the Florida Gators…loved to cook
chicken on the grill.

…got lost quite a few times but rarely admitted it; mooned a cruise
ship; found spiritual meaning in Jimmy Buffett songs; quoted
Abraham Lincoln daily; kept people at arm's length so he could see
them better; read "Siddhartha"…wrote poems to his wife…loved
listening to BB King, Albert King, Stevie Ray Vaughn, and Carlos
Santana play guitar…quoted Nelson Mandela; watched Field of
Dreams; named his son after his great grandfathers and George Brett;
went sledding down an icy mountain road; smoked his father's pipe;
read John Steinbeck's biography of Captain Henry Morgan…loved to
laugh at Chris Farley and John Belushi…had a few real good friends;
read two Hemingway biographies…loved beer; learned to like red
wine; listened to strangers…got the blues.

He read just about everything Carl Hiaasen's written, twice; stopped
going to Disneyworld after reading Hiaasen…built a deck; built
several decks; built a porch with a tin roof…He carved his name on a
channel marker by a mangrove island called Jackass Key. He liked to
be by himself; listened to what Bob Marley had to say; water--skied
behind a pickup truck……had a mutt named Summer—a great dog,
great friend…and a refugee Lab called Indie; another good friend.

He got grumpy; grew a beard; saw sea turtles offshore…bragged
about his kids; took his dogs by boat to the spoils islands in the
intracoastal… cried when the Steelers won the Super Bowl…had
hurricane parties; bought a 1973 Ford Bronco…listened to everything
John Wayne had to say. Lost a grandson.

…wore two dollar flip-flops…spent most of his life wearing flip-flops;
he wore cowboy boots for a while then went back to flip flops…
coached college baseball; named a boat "Plan B"…loved the Dave
Matthews Band; he once skipped work and went to Mass, skipped

Mass and went to the beach, several times…had fist-fights, and lost…once owned an old Jeep… took his kids out of school to go boating…he's been to Amelia Island, Pelican Island, Tybee Island, Merritt Island, Egmont Key, Little Torch Key, and Gainesville…and as James Taylor said, he always thought he'd see you again…

April 24

He didn't see her coming as he sat staring at his Guinness, arms folded across his chest. She tapped him on the shoulder as she slid onto the stool beside him.

"Well, what are you doing here?" Quinn said, smiling.

"You'll have to buy me one of those after I have this baby."

"That I will," Quinn promised.

"Anything good to eat around here?" she asked.

"Oh yeah, everything on the menu."

"Well, I read your work last night."

"I hope it didn't keep you up," Quinn said humbly.

Quinn ordered another Guinness and Jodi had a water with lemon…she looked over the menu…"What brings you downtown? He asked.

"Oh, I figured I'd find you here, on a Friday afternoon," Jodi replied.

After some small talk about school, the conversation took a turn.

"So, how do you think my father would feel about this? She asked. "I mean all I get from my mom these days are sighs…sighs over the phone."

"She doesn't live around here?" Quinn asked, playing dumb.

"No, thank God. Not quite sure I could handle that," she said.

Mothers and daughters. That was a whole different ballgame. Quinn knew enough not to go near it.

"I don't know, Jodi. I don't know," he said. "I think maybe…maybe he would feel like he failed you in some way. We're tough on ourselves like that." Again, there were spaces between Quinn's words.

After a pause, she asked, "How so?"

Quinn chose his words carefully. "By not instilling the importance of traditions...and..."

"And what," she cut him off..."morals?"

"No...not morals exactly." Quinn rubbed his head where his hair used to be. "I don't know, Jodi," he said again, softly and slowly. "There is great value in traditions...customs...ways of doing things." "They give us purpose. They give us roots...connections..." Quinn stopped then started again. "I'm afraid to live without them."

Jodi said, "You act like you've had experience with this."

"Oh I have," Quinn answered, stroking his beard, "which disqualifies me from giving any advice at all." He got the bartender's attention so she could order.

Jodi smiled and then sighed, "So Quinn, you're saying getting married would make my life easier?"

"No, it might make living easier...it won't make life easier,"

"So, do you talk this way to your students?" asked Jodi, breaking from the somber moment.

"What way?"

"Stopping, starting...you know, talking slowly, then pausing, leaving the listener hanging," she said. "It would drive me crazy!"

After a long pause, Quinn replied. "Yeah, I guess I do," laughing at himself.

Quinn eased back to the subject. "It's odd; I think you feel worse about your kids' struggles and missteps than your own."

"Well my mother has certainly expressed her disappointment with me," Jodi said with a certain amount of anger.

"Hmmm...maybe we see our own flaws and failings in our children," Quinn added. "My parents were pretty strict on my sisters and me, but I was in my mid-twenties when I found out that both of them were divorced before they met. I can't recall feeling less of them in any way...but for some reason they felt it important to keep it from us."

"How about when your kids screw up?" asked Jodi.

"Now that's a whole different story." Again, Quinn laughed at himself.

"How long have you been married?" she asked.

"Over thirty years," he answered.

"Don't be giving me some ballpark figure, how long?"

"Thirty three years," Quinn answered quickly.

Jodi pondered.

"Let me tell you, Jodi," said Quinn. "There's a whole lot I'm not sure about in this world, but I'm sure that if your dad could be here, he would be." "He would be here to love his daughter." "And your mom will be here when the time comes..."

She began to well up. "Have you told your kids everything you did?" she asked through tears.

"Hell no!" Quinn said laughing. "I was bad. When I get mad at my son or daughter, my wife is there to remind me of that fact oh too quickly...history, it's always here," he sighed.

Jodi laughed, drying her eyes.

"So what's this little girl's name going to be?" Quinn asked cheerfully.

"Stella," she said.

"Oh, that's purty," said Quinn. Every once in a while that Old Florida accent sneaked in. "Dave Matthews named one of his daughters Stella."

"You listen to Dave?" Jodi sounded surprised.

"Yeah…are you shocked?"

"A little," she said.

"How 'bout you?" Quinn asked.

"I love him."

"Hey, Dave's closer to my age than yours," he said. "And if you were thinking about asking me if I smoked weed, the answer's no, so get it out of your head!" They both laughed. "Anyway, Stella's a beautiful name. I can see her with wispy hair riding her tricycle around in circles."

"Wispy hair," Jodi repeated. "Sounds like something out of a memory."

She got up to leave. "Today's the Day, Quinn. Get your ass out of this bar and onto your boat."

A Few Things I've Learned

I was having this discussion just the other day and in trying to make a point, I described my observation as "objective." My friend jumped on the comment, questioning my ability to be a neutral observer of any sort. I admit I was taken back. I guess we'd all like to cloak ourselves in objectivity, but must passion always be taken for partisanship? And if we disagree, does that make your opinion skewed and biased? Is my differing opinion always driven by an ulterior motive or a political agenda?

Oftentimes, we are labeled by others for the sake of convenience. "I know where you stand." I don't know about you but I never felt comfortable with labels. My father was an Irish-Catholic Labor Union Democrat. My mother was a free-thinking conservative. My heroes have ranged from libertarians to bomb-throwing revolutionaries. To be sure, I'm, quick to play the devil's advocate, but my friends and family oftentimes wrongly assume my position on an issue. Why do you suppose that is?

Just as a leader can't lead from behind, a teacher can't teach from a perch upon the fence. Ideas are not just playthings of the mind. Ideas are not innocent, and they're definitely not all created equal. Teaching students to think for themselves doesn't require a teacher to check his views at the door. If you really wish to build democratic citizens, then you better be willing to get under their skin; to pull their chain; to press their buttons. The trick of course, is to do so with respect and tolerance and good humor.

Jefferson himself placed a bust of Hamilton in his foyer…a statue of his political adversary in his foyer. Although the two had been bitter political enemies, Jefferson lived long enough to realize the greatness of a man who possessed vastly different political views. "A difference of opinion," he wrote, "is not a difference in principle." Ronald Reagan chastised members of his staff for even using the word "enemy" in describing opposing party members.

We Americans are a curious lot. It's hard to pin down exactly who we are. But for the sake of debate, let's try.

Americans are **practical enough** to know that we can't fix anything with blanket policies. One size does not fit all!

Americans are **Jeffersonian enough** to grasp that liberty is a spiritual idea; and the purpose of freedom is to allow each and every one to find his or her own way.

They are **conservative enough** to embrace Edmund Burke's disdain for ideology and dogma.

...**liberal enough** to believe that there's more than one way to live.

...**educated enough** to believe in TR's Good Society...to understand the context of the Founders' principles...to appreciate the role of government in a complex industrial society. The snowball effect of urbanization and industrialization has altered the purpose of government within the realm of a democratic republic.

Americans are **moderate enough** to believe in "the middle way"

...**troubled enough** by the constant drone of pundits who claim we have betrayed our Founding Fathers' vision. Hell, the Founders themselves couldn't live up to such grand propositions. That's the wonder of it. They are our heroes — as men, not as gods.

Americans are **independent enough** to fear paternalism and the long range effects of institutionalized sympathy, but compassionate enough to concede the fact that our system has had a hand in creating the poverty we see in our country; and has a responsibility to find ways to relieve it.

They are **wise enough** to know that we are not always right. Sometimes we've been dead wrong. George Will said the spirit of liberty rests on the understanding that "I just might not be right." So, let's hear what you have to say.

Americans **remember enough** to know that laissez faire does not work in an industrial economy any better than socialist or corporatist central planning does. However, a policy of regulated markets and industries in no way disrespects the legacy of the Founders. It is a natural product of the social contract theory. I am not idealistic enough to believe that unregulated markets can work without causing serious long-term problems. As Republican Joe Scarborough said, *"There is nothing conservative about turning a blind eye to reckless speculation and greed."*

...**humble enough** to admit that they can be torn on moral issues. While we may have strong beliefs, there are times when each of us must say, "I just don't know."

...**patriotic and sensible enough** to embrace some economic nationalism. Companies and individuals who reap the benefits of our government policies should be willing to show gratitude and loyalty to this country.

Americans are **experienced enough** to realize that a market dominated by large corporations offers no more freedom than one controlled by an officious government. Some of America's greatest success stories are examples of how business and government can work together. The space program comes to mind.

...**unselfish enough** not to worry about who gets the credit in solving our problems. Many liberal ideas started in conservative think tanks...and vice versa...go figure.

Americans are **responsible enough** to answer the call to public service.

...**brash enough** to embrace American exceptionalism

They are **bewildered enough** by those who rant about the perverted sense of entitlement we Americans possess, while the ranters are the very products of such entitlement.

Americans are **awake enough** to see how Florence King's wisdom applies to both sides of the aisle: *"Democracy is the fig leaf of elitism."*

...**enlightened enough** to believe that the struggles of today are not necessarily for today (Lincoln). It will not be possible to curb government spending without addressing Social Security, Defense, and Health Care.

...**patriotic enough** to search for middle ground.

No civilization has taken democracy this far. I guess I believe we are as George Washington described: an experiment; a test said Lincoln...How free? How prosperous? Can it long endure? How far can we take this?

To say that we should not regulate goes against every notion of democratic society. We need traffic lights and litter laws, and even speed bumps. We need the FDA, the CDC, the EPA, the IRS, the SEC, the FDIC...for modern society to function, we need fire and police protection; public utilities; roads, bridges, dams; national parks; wildlife sanctuaries; social insurance; mosquito control; air traffic controllers; city transit...of course, we must be brave enough to do away with programs that don't work or have outlived their purpose.

Burke and Buckley both used the term **restraint** in describing conservatism; acknowledging society's duties and obligations, but also in serving the voice of reason. I believe it was Buckley who said that conservatism implied a submission to reality. But it seems to me that many of today's conservatives are falling victim to that which they detest most about liberals: **self-righteous ideological conformity.** One size does not fit all. And this is why I feel totally at ease shouting at my TV when politicians from the left **or** right start conjuring up the ghosts of Founders to suit their agendas.

How about *"bold persistent experimentation;"* or *"let's not fix what's not broken;"* or *"ask not what your country can do for you..."* Not as slogans but as courses of action.

FDR was the least ideological leader we've ever had. Of course, that's what made him successful. Only afterward — after he was gone — did his brand of liberalism become some sort of doctrine. At its best, welfare liberalism was tempered by fiscal restraint, and practiced (if not embraced) by conservatives such as Eisenhower and Nixon. History shows that JFK was probably more conservative as a Democrat than Nixon was as a Republican. Why ? I'm not sure. Maybe it's because both men were moderate...nonideological. Still, someone built a fence around welfare liberalism. Like New Right conservatism, it became a dogma. And the only moderation comes for the purpose of getting elected. Here we are.

April 28

"It's not like it's a secret around here," Jodi said out of the blue.

"What?"

"Your health issues," she said almost casually.

"You didn't know me, but you knew I had cancer?" Quinn was slightly irritated but not surprised it came up. "So is this the reason for your visits? You come down here to befriend a sick old man?"

"Oh, screw you, Quinn," she said softly. "I came down here for my own selfish reasons."

"I shouldn't have said that," Quinn replied. But he just stared down at the ants crawling across the bricks.

Jodi got up to leave and he stopped her. "Stay, please," he asked.

She turned.

"Okay, I had a touch of cancer."

"Touch of cancer?" Jodi asked.

"I heard Christopher Hitchens say that. I find it much more amusing now."

"Hilarious." Jodi sat back down.

"Part of you wants no one to know; part of you wants everyone to know. You think it's all about fighting to get your health back, but it takes even more than that. It robs you of your identity...your station. You're someone whose life now has an asterisk. *How are you doing* takes on a whole new meaning. It's no longer a cheerful, hollow salutation. People talk to you who never did before. Everyone treats you in the context of your illness. I'm not sure if our society can see past it. I had a lot of learning to do myself. A former student of mine sent me a Flannery O'Connor book when she heard I was ailing. She said:

"...sickness is a place more instructive than a long trip to Europe, and it's always a place where there's no company..."

"So Mr. Quinn, tell me about it." Jodi reached over and squeezed the back of his hand.

"Hodgkins Lymphoma Stage 2...found it in my right lung. No more cigars," he said. "Cuba's finally opening up and I have to quit cigars."

"Did you smoke a lot?" she asked.

"No, I was a real pedestrian," Quinn answered. "But I've got a little lung damage from the treatment, so I don't think it's a good idea...I'm not above sneaking one, though. To tell you the bare naked truth, Jodi, the treatment was tolerable. I had rough days. Maybe I have rough days ahead, who knows? But for the most part, I have been very lucky. Friends and family have been great...and I haven't had a lot of those *why me* moments. What's that line, suffering is redemptive."

"Unearned suffering is redemptive," she added. "King said that."

"Oh, I'm Irish Catholic," Quinn said. "We're not supposed to believe any suffering is unearned; or undeserved."

"I don't buy that," Jodi said.

"Pope John Paul II wrote a lot about the mystery of suffering," Quinn said with reverence. "He said it can cancel the just punishment for our misdeeds, it can provide humility, and even bring about a transformation."

"You seem to have read up on this quite a bit," she said.

"Oh, I have." Quinn went on to explain how bitter he was about his mother's suffering. "I was unable to comprehend it. Maybe my experiences will give me a little clarity after all these years. I'm thinking that's what Flannery O'Connor was talking about."

"Oh," she said," "you are so Catholic."

Quinn smiled. "Not a very good one, I'm afraid."

"Yeah, what's up with quoting Hitchens all the time?" Jodi asked. "He was a profound atheist."

"I'm a walking contradiction, ain't I?" Quinn said. "You gotta read things you disagree with, or your brain gets soft. Besides, he makes me stand on my own hind legs. Hitchens' arguments can strip you clean of all that is false…hope and faith are all that remain…and possible grace. He couldn't argue that out of me."

"Possible grace," he repeated.

"So everything's okay now?" she asked after a moment.

"As far as I know," he answered stoically. "Jodi, you know that overused Nietzsche quote, 'what does not kill you makes you stronger,' well it's no longer so quaint. It means something, now. I finally realized I've been blessed."

"How so?"

"Oh, I have many blessings, but among them, is the fact that for a long time I have been exactly where I should be," he said. "I've never been cursed with the desire to be somewhere else. *Be where you're at,* Michelle used to say."

"Michelle?" Jodi asked.

"She's the one who sent me the Flannery O'Connor book," Quinn answered.

"You seem to learn a lot from your students," said Jodi.

Quinn nodded and smiled.

"It does seem like everybody wants to be somewhere else." Jodi pondered. "It's like we're always afraid we're missing something."

"I know it drives some people crazy when I tell them that something doesn't have to be happening all of the time," Quinn replied.

Jodi agreed. "I love those times when nothing is really going on...what's that John Lennon line? Something like 'time enjoyed wasting isn't wasted,' or close to that."

"You know," Quinn said, "I thought about that when I was helping my son paint his house last weekend. There we were, spending a beautiful day mired in the tedium of painting, but there was good music, cold beer, good company...it was a good day."

"How did we end up talking about painting?" Jodi asked.

Culture

I cannot recall the first time I didn't feel like a tourist in my own culture. I don't remember what finally gave me a sense of connection to the ways of life around me. It was no epiphany, I can assure you. Maybe it was more like John Hiatt said, "a slow turning."

Like so many Americans, I spent years on the outside looking in. Experiencing America — aside from my own fragmented subculture — was like going to Homecoming and sitting in the corner, watching other people dance. I could hear the music, but I couldn't feel it.

So, what was it that pulled me in? Was it hearing the Blues in Van Morrison? Was it Wynton Marsalis opening my eyes by likening Jazz — and America — to a rich gumbo? Could it have been my father's stories of the Irish in America; or Gerald Early's memory of young blacks singing the Star Spangled Banner at an inner city sandlot baseball game?

Here I was, a product of all this; an Irish-Catholic descendant of 20th Century urban America. You know the one; the patchwork of ethnic neighborhoods sewn into industrial Northern cities. But I was no city-dweller and by no means a Northerner. And on the other side, my Florida roots reached deep into south Alabama and Georgia. I came along years after the family made an exodus to a once sleepy little town on the east coast of Florida.

My family brought to the Jim Crow South an urban Pittsburgh Irish and a dark rural New Hampshire to go along. We were thrown into the mix with Georgians and New York Italians. A family of Cuban exiles lived one street over; Boston liberals across the street, next to some renters from Alabama, or was it Mississippi? Our next door neighbors were refugees from Kentucky coal mines.

Despite the subtle blending of folkways and customs, most were oblivious to roots or heritage. I remember a West Virginian kid getting into a hell of a fight over which side his home state was on in the Civil War. He went home crying when he found out he was a Yankee! Now I'm not sure we had our history straight in 1965, but when it got right down to it, our culture was a whiteness defined only as "nonblack."

Now don't get me wrong, I grew up with a great appreciation for the ways of the South, to the point that it annoyed my father. As only he would say, "just because a cat has kittens in the oven, it don't make 'em muffins." When I was very young, my sister married a guy who traced his Florida roots back to the nineteenth century, and he did his best to instill as many Southern traditions in me as possible.

The Italian-American family across the street nurtured their heritage. They even cussed at each other in Italian. And my family's ethnicity was so thick you could cut it with a knife. We celebrated being Irish at every turn. Although my friends' perceptions of the Irish were almost cartoon-like, I was always made to feel unique and blessed to be who I was. But even before the ways of the immigrants got to me, the "Irish" was stewed in America. In this place where everything is influenced by everything else, I was in the soup. I was not Irish, but Irish-American.

Still, with the passion for culture and the interest in all of the gumbo's ingredients, there sometimes comes the assumption that some groups are devoid of unique traits and traditions. A longing for the richness of "other folks' culture" is somehow construed as a admission that yours is bland and unexciting. Perhaps it was sanitized by the onslaught of generations raised and educated to believe one can only celebrate his roots if he is oppressed. Otherwise, *you're being ethnocentric, so knock it off!* This was a notion that ethnicity was a barrier to acceptance and tolerance.

This tendency to suppress cultural differences among white ethnic groups was born of good intentions, but it is in fact a perversion of the Civil Rights movement. When Justice John Harlan said that *the Constitution is color blind,* he was talking about a person's rights before the law. It was not some manifesto on dissolving all cultural differences in America. On the contrary Harlan recognized that it was human nature to have preferences and prejudices, and the law must be created and applied so that nothing obstructs the opportunities and protections of each citizen. Equality does not require an individual to be stripped of all that gives him identity: his race, creed, color, gender…

Out of some sense of political accountability, many ethnic groups among the white majority don't nurture their cultural traditions. Along with losing those things that are vital to our identity, some may also lose their appreciation for culture itself, as an essential force of cohesion in our society. Taking down that flag in South Carolina is more complicated than just taking down a flag in South Carolina. And it should be.

The very nature of culture in America has been one of diffusion. We can't help but influence each other. We spread our traits and adapt other people's traits to our way of life. If you don't think I'm right, go to someone else's church. It's a whole different ballgame.

I don't want to lose my Irish any more than latinos or blacks want to lose their heritage. But a big step toward knocking down racial and ethnic barriers is to grasp how we influence each other. Teaching students about Jazz is much more than celebrating the awakening of Black culture. Jazz — a unique product of cultural diffusion — could only be born in America. It exemplifies *American culture.*

If the *gumbo* analogy doesn't work for you, how about the *quilt?* Before the blanket can be made, many pieces of cloth must first be gathered. They are sewn together to form a beautiful patchwork. Again, the individual must first discover her own identity before finding her connection to the group.

Ideally, I want my students to glance over to their right and then to their left, and see people with much in common, but also with distinct differences. We're not after Gray Street, so to speak. I don't think that's equality. Dissolving differences is not necessarily the way to eliminate bias.

I want my students to feel their uniqueness. I try to find out about their backgrounds. We do several "Ellis Island" projects so students can discover their own stories. The desks in my classroom are filled with all sorts — a Persian kid; the Latina from the Bronx; the Japanese boy; the Irish girl; a Texan; the descendant of African slaves; the granddaughter of Cuban exiles; and the fourth generation Floridian.

But no one gets a special parking place. We're not after particularism, or separatism. We have to discover what connects us by first finding what distinguishes us. It's a slippery slope these days with so many feelings so easily hurt. In a society filled with thin skin, a teacher is walking a very fine line when he discusses race or culture. Racism in this country is a wound that will not heal. It scabs over, only to bleed again at the slightest altercation. Religion? Forget about it. We may be more sensitive about religion than we are about race.

Of course, the easy way to deal with culture is to ignore it. Let's not talk about it at all. Let's pretend that there is no such thing as race or religion. Let's pretend that none of these issues are carried into the classroom.

It is no great revelation that culture creates societies. The total pattern of human behavior and its products become the glue of society. This *gathered up way of life;* this gradual accumulation of traits plays a unique role in the American story. With so many different groups flooding into this place, the blending of culture is going on without our consent. Whether we like it or not, we are all continuously influencing each other through our language, values, lifestyle, music, and even food.

Therein lies the paradox; how do we nurture our own unique histories and also accept cultural diffusion as a driving force in our society? If we reject this force of cohesion and fight for a fragmented society that lashes out against forces of unity as repugnant to cultural and racial integrity, are we not walking down a treacherous road? Are we following Europe's legacy of cultural separatism and ethnocentric nationalism?

May 1

"A girl told me the other day that you were mean."

"Yeah, I get that a lot these days," Quinn replied, wondering where in the hell was this going.

"She said you're very sarcastic," Jodi probed.

"Ha! They don't even get sarcasm! Some of my best stuff falls on deaf ears and open mouths."

"Well, this girl got it," she said. "...did you really say, *giving you the right to vote was like giving her a Barnes and Noble gift card?*"

Quinn sneered and crossed his arms. "Well your Honor, I'll take the Fifth on that one."

Jodi crossed her arms, mimicking his gesture.

"If you have high expectations of someone," said Quinn, "and he or she consistently falls short, surely frustration is bound to set in. For years, I've found humor to be a much more effective weapon than other indignities I could inflict. Sermons and scoldings have their place but sometimes the only thing that works is a little sarcasm. That's the way it used to be, at least, but these days..."

"A lot of kids can't handle it," she said.

"No shit, Jodi. I'll admit that I am brutally intolerant of laziness and apathy, and I will rip you a new one if that's what you give me. I always try to build them back up again." Quinn was unapologetic. Still, he took care to soften his tone.

"A lot of those kids have shit going on at home you wouldn't believe."

Quinn put up his hand. "Please. We send the wrong message when we give a kid a free pass just because his home life is messed up."

"This isn't the Quinn I heard about."

He winced at her remark and then continued. "These days, when I call them out; when I get onto them; when I chew them out; there seems to be no effect anymore. I'm just a grumpy old guy who doesn't like kids."

"To be honest Quinn, maybe you come across that way sometimes."

"I try to raise the expectations they have for themselves," he said defensively. "Seems like I'm failing at that lately."

Jodi backed off. "Did something happen recently?"

"I was going to ask the same question." The answer was yes, but Quinn was in no mood to vent...especially in this atmosphere.

He tried to deflect things by asking Jodi about her Dr.'s appointment.

"Yeah, everything's fine," she said. "What's up with you?"

"Not much," he said elusively. Their conversation had come to a grinding halt.

"How's the baby's room coming along?" Before she could answer, Quinn was up and headed for the parking lot. "Wait here, I just remembered I have something for you." Quinn returned quickly. In his hand was a CD of lullabies by Dave Matthews.

Jodi forgot all about their tense discussion they had a few minutes before. "This is so cool! You know, Mr. Quinn, you're alright."

"Yeah," Quinn said, "I'm alright."

A Teachable Moment

A teachable moment. I never cared for that phrase, but it fits. A few years back, I met some friends at *Meg O'Malley's* to partake in a little March Madness. The Gators were making a run in the NCAA playoffs and so we had gathered to root them on.

I was dressed in my customary shabby chic apparel for a Florida March: flannel shirt, cargo shorts, baseball cap, and flip flops. It was Friday night as I recall and the place was pretty crowded — three deep at the bar. It was loud, as you can imagine, with 200 people all trying to talk over an Irish band and beer-drinking basketball fans.

When I dashed to the men's room during a timeout, I found the usual bottleneck, but as I waited my turn, I sensed there was something else going on. A white gentleman with a thick Boston accent was standing at the urinal, having a conversation over his shoulder with a black gentleman at the sink.

The exchange sounded pleasant enough until the Boston guy commented on the black guy's choice of beverage, which he apparently brought into the bathroom. "You got your Hennessy, I see," he said, and it apparently struck a nerve. "Oh, just because I am a black man," he said while drying his hands, "you assume that I drink a certain drink? You think that all African-Americans drink the same thing?"

Remember, this is an Irish bar, and this sociology moment sucked the air right out of the room (bad image, I know). Anyway, there's five or six white guys with absolutely nothing to say. All I wanted to do was get back to the basketball game.

Later on in the evening, when we were leaving, I returned to the bathroom before heading home (what can I say, I'm over 50). This time there was only one other guy in there and as luck would have it, it was the black gentleman. And somehow he recognized me from the earlier encounter. I nodded politely and tried to make it to the door, but he headed me off at the pass. "I want to apologize, sir, for my earlier outburst," he said. "It's just I've been fighting stereotypes all my life."

Now I'm not sure what he'd been drinking, but it was apparent that he had quite a few by this time. The man began to speak of entirely too much for a men's room conversation and I was getting fidgety. It really got awkward when he began to recite a line of poetry. I recognized the verse, and smilingly said, "Langston Hughes." He stepped back and took measure of me from head to toe — baseball cap to flip flops — and finally said, "You know Langston Hughes?"

As soon as the words came out of his mouth, a look of incredulity came over his face. We both laughed, and finally, went our separate ways.

May 11

"I have a sister. She lives in Miami."

"Really?" Quinn said with a bit of surprise in his voice. "I thought you were an only child."

"She's a dancer," Jodi added.

"That's cool," Quinn said, unsure of where this was headed.

"Not that kind of dancer, Quinn. She's a stripper. My sister's a stripper."

"Oh…"

"We don't talk much," Jodi said. "She and my mom don't talk at all. I don't think they've spoken since my dad's funeral."

"Sorry to hear that," Quinn said, stammering. "…about you 'all not talking. You don't have to be telling me this other stuff, though, Jodi."

"I'm telling you."

"I'm not sure why." Quinn wondered if she was testing him in some way. He searched in vain for the right words. "My dad taught me to respect all women, regardless of their station…he said life is harder for women, so don't judge them."

Jodi seemed ready for his piece of wisdom and fired back. "Would you be thinking that if it were your sister, or daughter?"

"No," he said rather quickly. "And I'm pretty sure I wouldn't be telling you about it.

Both of them sat for several moments without speaking.

Quinn broke the silence. *"We are more wicked and flawed, Jodi, than we ever imagined and more loved and accepted than we dare to hope.* A guy named Tim Keller said that. Got it from a student...I think it was Cheyenne...or Nathan..." Quinn scratched the back of his head. "Was it Alyse?"

"Does it matter?" Jodi asked.

"Yes, it does...very much so."

Again, she reached over and placed her hand on top of his.

Heroes and the Trial of History

You never have the last word on history, and a teacher doesn't have to act like he does. When revelations appear that challenge our traditional notions, or when stories surface altering our view of a particular character, it should only serve to bolster our interest in the remarkable events in the history of our republic.

The real hazard lies in how we approach telling the story in the first place. If we stay true and try to present figures in history as first and foremost human, then our heroes become even more valuable to us. But if we paint a picture of our leaders as gods— prophets of stone who are divinely inspired to lead the masses— then we are setting ourselves up for failure and confusion.

When a student discovers news of Jefferson's hypocrisy, FDR's deceit, or Kennedy's recklessness, the resulting disillusionment may blind her to the real human heroism we find in each. If we take away their flaws—their humanity—they offer little of use to the student. How can we hope for the emergence of new leaders? How can anyone measure up to hero-gods? But when we discover that America's giants actually had feet of clay, it can allow each of us to see the potential for achievement deep within our flawed selves.

Sometimes I wish I could launder the history of Jefferson or Jackson. I cannot. As much as he fears that the negative side of their stories will muddy up the student's perspective of our heroes, the teacher must trust the truth. And by the truth I mean the whole story, scratches and dents included. If I've presented my entire course with the focus on human nature, then I must have faith in giving students as much as I have and let them judge for themselves. The American who emerged from the Revolution was flawed but perfectible, and capable of extraordinary things. That's how we should present our heroes.

FDR's rise from a shallow, ambitious empty suit of a politician, through devastating illness, to an indispensible figure in American History, is inspiring. The effect of Kennedy's health on his political and personal behavior is an intriguing story. Robert E. Lee's story of a virtuous man stuck in impossible circumstances can awaken us to the terrible complexities of public life, and alter our understanding of courageous leadership.

Still, it's strange how we are very protective of some, while others are targets of countless investigations into their character, deeds, and misdeeds. Theodore Roosevelt immediately comes to mind. TR is one of my favorite characters in history. My students love to hear about him.

Few men exemplify modern America like Theodore Roosevelt. If Franklin and Jefferson were our renaissance men, and Lincoln was our prophet, then Roosevelt was a force of nature. He pushed America into world leadership. For the first time, modern social and economic problems were addressed by a republican government, and it was done on his watch. Here was a man whose actions matched his words. His rhetoric and leadership not only helped change the role of government, but also created what we think of as the modern presidency. As the most popular president ever, TR raised the stature of the office itself.

For many years — most of my career, actually — I taught the legend, as John Wayne said. I taught TR's story without looking behind the curtain myself. I took great pains to learn and teach the human sides of Washington, Jefferson, Lincoln, and FDR, but I continued to present a Theodore Roosevelt that was an icon only. If flaws of other leaders had added to their appeal, TR was an exception. His heroism kept pushing him further and further above reproach.

He was larger than life for me. Every biography I read, every new story I heard raised my opinion of him. War hero. Consumer advocate. Protector of the environment. Civil Rights supporter...

For some reason, Roosevelt's flaws were all but invisible, or at least harmless. We presented his politics without criticism, and I can assure you, there was plenty of room for it. We seem less troubled and more amused by Roosevelt's excesses. It's safe to say that historians and professors have fallen in love with TR, and I was certainly guilty myself.

I can't think of a better example than how Roosevelt's opponents were portrayed by historians. For decades scholars accepted TR's own assessment of his adversaries. *They were laissez-faire conservatives who greatly distrusted popular government.* Through my own intellectual laziness, I accepted this view of early conservatism as gospel. As mainstream scholars embraced Charles Beard's *Economic Interpretation of the Constitution* and the argument that the Constitution was crafted to protect wealthy interests, they promoted a negative opinion of any opponents of 20th century progressivism.

In reality, conservatives like William Howard Taft fully understood the need for a strong national government to check the excesses of modern industrial capitalism. However, they had a real problem with "constitutional progressivism" — a radical reform program Roosevelt adopted during his efforts to reclaim the presidency in 1912.[60]

Garry Wills' *Inventing America* had long since challenged Beard's cynical view of the Founders, and I was very much on board with that, but a few years back, I stumbled upon a paper written by William Schambra that knocked me for a loop. Its central focus was on the Election of 1912 and the dramatic attempt by Theodore Roosevelt to reshape the US Constitution. I had been teaching about the 1912 election for decades. How could this have escaped me? I checked every textbook, new and old, and I could not find mention of this action. I began to scour the bookshelves.

After four years out of office, Roosevelt was persuaded that his monumental legislative program could not survive without fundamental constitutional changes. In 1912, TR unveiled a plan to overcome "structural obstacles to change"[61]

Roosevelt's long struggles against money power had left him open to suggestions that the Constitution was being used as a force against progressive reform. Schambra went so far as to describe the

---

[60] In William A. Schambra, "The Origins and Revival of Constitutional Conservatism: 1912 and 2012" *First Principles* Series Report #44 on *Political Thought. (Washington DC: Heritage Foundation). Retrieved from http://www.heritage.org/research/reports/2012/08/the-origins-and-revival-of-constitutional-conservatism-1912-and-2012*

[61] Ibid.

struggles within the Republican Party as a struggle with the question of democracy and the Constitution itself.[62]

A voracious reader, TR was ultimately convinced by J. Allen Smith's *The Spirit of American Government,* which even predates Beard. Smith claimed that the Founders had deliberately constructed a government to "thwart majority rule." On February 1, 1912, Roosevelt gave a rousing speech in Columbus, Ohio called *A Charter for Democracy,* where he outlined a progressive constitutional program. In an effort to make elected representatives accountable to to the people's will, Roosevelt's plan included:

- Initiative, referendum, and recall...including recall of judges
- Direct election of Senators
- Popular recall of judicial decisions

His struggles with corporate interests led him to believe that the barriers to public will must be torn down, even if it required fundamental changes in the Constitution[63]

In August of 1912, after failing to capture the Republican nomination, TR formed his own party and accepted its nomination with another stirring speech, *A Confession of Faith.* In that speech, Roosevelt called for "a new contract with the people," arguing that new government powers required new rights for citizens.[64] He had bought into the myth being permeated by contemporary intellectuals like Smith and Beard that *the scheme of government* had to be changed. They argued that the Founders wanted to check democracy by building a Constitution with major obstacles to the people's will. By casting a shadow over the Founders' motives, *some* progressives sought to weaken the resistance to democratic reforms of the Constitution.

---

[62] Ibid.

[63] Jean Yarbrough. *Theodore Roosevelt and the American Political Tradition, (Lawrence:* University Press of Kansas, 2012)

[64] Ibid.

In truth, James Madison had made no bones about limiting democracy. Majorities had to be checked just as stringently as any other potential tyranny. His Constitution brilliantly moderated those tendencies.

Through some thorough detective work, Garry Wills challenged the revisionist myths surrounding the Framers of the Constitution. Beard's economic thesis is undermined by the simple demographics of the Philadelphia Convention. If the Constitution was in fact crafted to defend the rich minority against the masses, why were the seven men who walked out of the Convention among the richest in America? Why was it that the three states that unanimously ratified the Constitution were controlled by farm interests? Why was the opposition to the Constitution led by men who already held power and privilege in the states? [65]

The Federalists—those supporting the Constitution—were *the young guns*. They were men of the younger generation. Men like John Marshall and Alexander Hamilton were greatly influenced by their Revolutionary War experiences. They fought alongside Washington and saw many of his efforts frustrated by a weak and ineffective government. The Federalists were on the average eleven years younger than the Anti-Federalists; four of the nine Federalist leaders were still in their twenties at the time of the Philadelphia Convention[66].

To be sure, Theodore Roosevelt saw his opponents as cynically using the veneration of the Founding Fathers to obstruct his legislative program, and certainly there were some who did just that. But many of his friends, supporters, and even family members withdrew their support in 1912 when his politics shifted radically. As sophisticated as TR was, it seems rather curious that he would ultimately embrace populism. But there was great power in populism, and Roosevelt knew that.

---

[65]Wills, *Inventing America,* 354.

[66] Ibid.

"…allow the people at large to override the monstrous perversion of the Constitution into an instrument for the perpetuation of social and industrial wrong and for the oppression of the weak and helpless."

-Theodore Roosevelt[67]

The most radical proposal in Roosevelt's package of constitutional reforms was the recall of judicial decisions. Schambra claimed that TR was fully aware of its implications. Judicial recall "would give the power of the majority to change the fundamental meaning of the Constitution."[68] Roosevelt didn't stop there. He also advocated a change in the amendment process which would allow simple majorities to alter the Constitution.

Many Republicans supported Roosevelt's bid to regain the presidency, but after the "Charter" speech, they turned against him. Senator Elihu Root, a fervent supporter of TR's domestic program as member of his cabinet, separated himself after the speech. He was deeply disturbed by Roosevelt's attack on the moderating influences in the Constitution. Root eloquently defended the practical wisdom of the Founders:

"In our Constitution…we have set up a barrier against ourselves. As Ulysses required his followers to bind him
to the mast that he might not yield to the song of the siren…so the American democracy has bound itself to the great rules of right…"[69]

Roosevelt's life-long friend Henry Cabot Lodge had also spoken on the danger of constitutional progressivism as far back as early 1911. He believed that no law or policy was important enough to damage the Constitution. When he read Roosevelt's "Charter" speech, Lodge put his friendship aside and broke with TR.

---

[67]TR, "A Charter of Democracy: Address Before the Ohio Constitutional Convention, February 21, 1912, http://www.theodore-roosevelt.com/images/research/txtspeeches/704.pdf.

[68] Schambra.

[69] Elihu Root quoted in Schambra.

The noble defense of the Constitution against the progressive onslaught is all but forgotten. As I said before, in no textbook did I find any mention of the constitutional struggles of 1912. We speak of this election as a prime example of party realignment, and we use it to explain the effects of a splinter party, but nowhere do we discuss the huge constitutional implications of 1912.

> "If Roosevelt failed to win the hearts and minds
> of Republicans in 1912, it seems that he has nonetheless won
> the hearts of professors ever since."
> -William Schambra[70]

We history teachers slam Woodrow Wilson's progressive policies because of his hostility toward civil liberties and women's rights, but Wilson never moved on the Constitution. We rip FDR for his court-packing scheme, but Franklin Roosevelt never suggested changes that would break down checks and balances. TR's actions, however, have gone generally unnoticed...or at least unmentioned.

So where do we go from here? Roosevelt's political shift is troubling. He had resisted and even condemned radical populism throughout his career. But the immense popularity "Teddy" enjoyed may have skewed his judgment. Even in his retirement, we see the intoxicating dangers of power. After all Roosevelt was human.

As for me, revelations of Theodore Roosevelt's faults and missteps do nothing to lessen my admiration for him. They do, however, put him back into perspective. We can never lose sight of the human side of our heroes. Without it they are no good to us. The lesson learned here is that just as there are extremely ordinary aspects to a hero's character, there may well be extraordinarily heroic aspects to our own.

---

[70] Schambra.

May 15

It had been a few days since Jodi had visited. Quinn worried that he had run her off. The last conversation they had had been dark, so dark that maybe she had decided she had enough of this. He had only come down to the bench once in the past week and she was nowhere to be found.

Jodi was speaking of her father on that day and the grief that had haunted her. Old Quinn was all too familiar with that. He had offered her some wisdom and comfort:

"Sorrow, like the wind, comes in gusts."

"I like that," she said after a moment. "Is that you?"

"No, no, it's Marjorie Kinnan Rawlings," Quinn answered. "Good Florida writer."

Jodi took a sip from her bottle of water and then said slowly, "A couple of weeks ago, when we were talking about rocking chairs, you spoke of your wife in present tense."

"Yeah," Quinn answered matter-of-factly. "Funny how that happens."

"I didn't know you lost her," she said with all the sympathy she could muster.

"I did," he said. "Five years ago this month."

"You did it another time, too." She said gently. "I think we were talking about..."

"It doesn't matter. I do it all the time. Everybody thought I would lose my mind...maybe I have," he said with a smile...a sad one. "Living without her is like walking around with one boot on. People — good people — will say *'you should see someone, Frank, get some help,'* but I tell 'em I'm not depressed. I just miss her."

The evenings were the toughest. The time they set aside for each other was now the time he set aside for remembering. They would sit and talk; debate; argue; reminisce…plan vacations. Unlike most couples, their relationship had maintained structure even through three decades. Regardless of what was going on in their lives, they kept to their rituals. Dinnertime was always a time of conversation and discussion. The two were intellectual equals, and they loved to spar over the issues of the day. The news of nations filled their talk.

Jean was able to retire while Quinn continued to work. She loved the thought of being a grandmother…"Yes, sorrow comes in gusts."

"And you lost a grandson?" Jodi asked with the leverage of an expectant mother.

Why was she asking him these questions? Why was she stirring up these memories?

"Yes, Jodi," Quinn answered. "I don't want to talk about that. Everybody's got burdens to shoulder and now you know mine.

"I'm sorry, Quinn, I don't even know why I asked that."

Jodi ran her fingers through her hair. Again she apologized.

Quinn looked straight ahead. "I cannot for the life of me figure out how and why you came along." Then he got up and walked away.

"Did it ever occur to you," she called out, "that I feel the same way?"

"No," she heard him say.

It was nearing the end of the school year and Quinn thought perhaps she would use that as a way of breaking the habit of visitations, but here she came, walking slowly down the steps.

"Here, you forgot this," she said, handing him a book. "You left it on the bench the other day."

"Thanks, Jodi, did you read any of it?" he asked.

"No, Mr. Quinn, Hemingway isn't my favorite," she said offhandedly. Quinn always carried a book to the bench so he could act surprised to see her. He never wanted to appear as if he took her visits for granted. Today, though, he was genuinely surprised.

"I thought I ran you off," he said.

"Are you kidding? I thought I ran *you* off," she answered, still sounding apologetic. "I was out of line."

He had no answer.

"I'm really jammed with end of the year," she said, taking the conversation in a different direction."...and I'm taking time off with the baby coming. What's the best way to get hold of you, email?"

Quinn was pleased with the question. "Either that or text message. Here's my number."

Jodi typed it into her phone, resisting the impulse to check her messages. "Be where you're at," she said softly.

"Pardon?" he said.

"Nothing, just talking to myself," said Jodi. "Quinn, I've been meaning to ask you, what does *coke bottle green* water look like?

"What?"

"When you were talking about the Gulf, you described the water as coke bottle green."

Quinn laughed. "Ha! I'm showing my age! You don't remember the old glass Coke bottles?" he asked.

"Nope."

"Well," he said, "I'll have to work on my imagery. Jimmy Buffett said don't try to describe the ocean if you've never seen it...and even then we fall short. Coke bottle green...let's see, it's not sage," Quinn said. "gray-green...slate, maybe... I love Hemingway because he takes the time to describe what things look like...smell like... taste like..."

"Yeah, I'll give him that," said Jodi.

" You have to be a noticer," old Quinn reminded her.

May 22

Frank Quinn was a notoriously bad driver. He was skilled enough, but the insane pace of Florida's highways drove him to distraction. 70% of the population was from somewhere else, and Quinn was convinced that Florida attracted the worst drivers in the United States. Of course, he saw nothing wrong with his own abilities. Jean used to say, "Frank, just because you're a native Floridian doesn't mean you always have the right of way." Quinn thought that might be a good idea and gave it entirely too much consideration. Maybe even a special bumper sticker would be good.

He did battle his own impatience, though. He plainly saw the irony in never being in a hurry until he was behind the wheel. He'd putter around the house for two hours, then suddenly realize he had to be to work in fifteen minutes. The traffic on 192 was maddening, and it seemed to be getting worse every day. Quinn would shake his head as he waited for a break, remembering his grandfather's prophesy. Finally, he'd make the left turn toward school right into the sunrise.

When he got to his classroom, there were a couple of students waiting. One had a question and the other wanted to know if she could store her soccer gear in his room. Quinn turned on his music and checked his email.

Email:

8:05 Jodi: Good Morning

8:20 Jodi: Helllooo?

8:31 Quinn: Good Morning. How are you feeling?

8:43 Jodi: Bleh…didn't sleep much…read an interesting article, though…reminded me of your Hemingway obsession.

8:50 Quinn: Hemingway obsession?

9:42 Jodi: Will you be heading down to the bench today? I'll tell you about it.

10:26 Quinn: Uh, I have to sneak home and let the dogs out. My daughter can't make it over today, so…

11:27 Jodi: No worries, Mr…see you whenever

The sky fell out around one o'clock, so a bench visit was out of the question, anyway. Quinn waited for the rain to let up and then slipped out the side gate and headed home. The dogs were happy to see him, but he had to turn right back around and go back to work. When he returned, there was an email waiting.

1:15 Jodi: Like I said, when I entered the profession, I thought every day was going to be a scene out of *Dead Poet's Society*, minus the suicide and Keating's dismissal, of course. I would be inspiring students, pushing them farther than they'd ever gone before, and in turn, they would stand on their desks, and I would be a legend. Oddly, it didn't go that way. Instead, I made a bunch of bonehead rookie mistakes, let the kids get away with murder, and vacillated between trying to push them to work harder and trying to push them to like me more. I don't think I was mature enough to accomplish what I'd set out to. But this year… This year something has shifted. I've let my nerd flag fly more than ever, and I've worried less about winning them over and more about getting them where they need to be—and oddly, I feel like I have created stronger relationships AND maintained higher expectations than I've been able to before. I've yet to see someone stand on a desk, but…

1:37 Quinn: What happened to that article you were going to tell me about?

1:43 Jodi: Stay with me.

3:25 Jodi: The trust I've built this year has been incredible and I think it's because I finally made myself a bit more vulnerable. I've shared pics, stories from high school, confessed to insecurities, and fessed up when I didn't have the right answer on a practice test, or didn't know the meaning of a word. I'm trying to marry my love of reading and talking about books with my love of performing, and laughter, and growth… my identities with my intellectual ambitions and passions. I'm letting it all hang out and it seems to be working. At the very least, I'm having a great time. I'm excited to be here, excited to come to work…and now this…a baby.

Quinn sat back and reread Jodi's last message. "Whew," he said to an empty room. "This girl is something." … *marry my love of reading and talking about books with my love of performing, and laughter, and growth…my identities with my intellectual ambitions and passions.* For the first time in a long while, he felt good about the future of his profession.

May 26

"So how was your Memorial Day weekend, Mr. Quinn?" Jodi said from the foot of the stairs.

"Pretty good, Ms. Richardson, pretty good. How was yours?"

"Nice," she said. "Got to meet with a priest and discuss a few things."

"Wait a minute, you're Catholic? But..."

"Yes, Quinn. My Catholicism has been a lot like your cigar smoking – pedestrian. But things have changed."

Quinn smiled and shook his head. "Never heard it put quite like that. So what was that article you were going to tell me about the other day?"

"Actually, it was an interview with this brain scientist who had a stroke. She wrote a book about it.

"This sounds familiar," Quinn said.

"She couldn't talk or walk or anything. Her rehab took like eight years. But after she recovered, she described this sense of well-being she felt while being held captive by her own body."

"Jill Taylor."

"Don't tell me you've heard of her."

"Jodi, I used this story the last time I taught Psych."

"No way."

"She talks about *push* and *pause?*" Quinn asked.

"Damn it, Quinn. You have heard of her." Jodi elbowed him. "Yeah, she said once you realize you have two brains you can learn to switch from one hemisphere to another and control your life from moment to moment."

Quinn nodded his head and said something about the left side being focused on the past and future, while the right side is more concerned with the present.

"And if you're feeling stressed," Jodi said, "you can get out of it by paying attention to your senses. In other words, zoom in on the smells and sights and sounds around you and that will pull you out of the mental clutter, over to a place where you're aware of the richness of the moment. Anyway, I thought about that look you get when you talk about Hemingway."

"Don't wanna go all Hemingway on you." They both laughed.

"So maybe this is why writing is so liberating — you're forced to focus upon the here and now. Right hemisphere stuff. What do you think?"

Quinn shrugged, "Be where you're at." Maybe there's something to it."

One True Line

On Hemingway, Conroy, and Plato

"*Otro loco mas,*
said the barman and turned away."
-Ernest Hemingway
from *A Clean Well Lighted Place*[71]

Yes, I am another crazy one. I sit in the shadows of the café. They are shadows from the tree against the light. It's late and I can feel the quiet. I will lie in bed tonight, and maybe with daylight, I will fall asleep.

I think it was Jim Harrison who said that good stories make him want to live inside them. That's how it is with me. More often than not, it's Hemingway, Pat Conroy, or Harrison himself. I can pick up Hemingway and find one particular line that envelops my mood. Each paragraph, each sentence seems to stand on its own. I am at once captivated by a setting or description. I am transfixed by the passing impressions of a character. A familiar passage blows across my face like the first time I read it.

Plato claimed in *the Allegory of the Cave* that enlightenment must be learned and requires a mentor. Ernest Hemingway has been one of mine. To Plato, light is truth, and Hemingway tried to tell the whole truth—to hold back nothing. He said that he was compelled to give an account of things, or "the way it truly happened, the ecstasy and sorrow, remorse and how the weather was…"[72] I love to drop in on passages of books I've read several times before, like page 35 of

[71] Ernest Hemingway, *The Complete Short Stories of Ernest Hemingway* (New York: Charles Scribner's Sons/MacMillan Publishing Company, 1987), 291.

[72] Ibid., *A Moveable Feast.* New York: Touchstone, 1992.

Old Man and The Sea, where he describes the ocean as he moves offshore.

Hemingway once said that each man's life begins and ends the same, so then, it is the *details* in between that distinguish one person from another. Perhaps he is not alluding to achievement, but to experience. When I read Hemingway, I know the *details*- the taste of the food, the smells of the sea, and the yearnings and dreads of the men and the women who live and die in his books. It is here that he assumes the role of a teacher. In Plato's journey, it's necessary to return to the community after one sees the light. The steps toward enlightenment do not involve seeking a new world, but seeing the old world differently. Hemingway's work reveals his ability to see. As an artist, he allows us to recognize things for what they really are. Thus, he has fulfilled his duty by showing the truth to others.

> There are some things which cannot be learned
> quickly, and time, which is all we have, must be
> paid heavily for their acquiring. They are the
> very simplest things and because it takes a man's
> life to know them the little new that each man gets
> from life is very costly and the only heritage
> he has to leave.   --Hemingway
>   from *A Moveable Feast*[73]

Hemingway's work endures. To this day, he shows me the shadows, the reflections, the light, and the darkness.

> *On a day that was stolen*
> *From the seeds I have sown-*
> *With time that was borrowed*
> *On a boat I half own;*
> *Beneath a sky that was given*
> *In a mood I had found,*
> *I tried to write one true line…*
> *JM*

---

[73] Ibid., Moveable Feast.

June 2

"Chautauqua," he repeated.

Jodi read from her phone: *various traveling shows and local assemblies of the late 19th century providing popular education and entertainment – modeled after the Chautauqua Institute of southwestern New York.*

"Are you pulling my leg?"

"No," said Quinn. "It's a narrative lecture, a conversation if you will, always with pertinent digression. I first heard Shelby Steele use the term."

Jodi brushed the hair away from her forehead.

"You stand up there with a cup of coffee or tea and tell stories," Quinn continued.

Jodi crossed her arms.

"Look, no one is absolutely sure how to measure learning, anyway. They think they know, but if they did, why do they keep changing their methods every other year? Good stories don't teach kids what to think, but how to think."

"I think I've heard you say that before," she said.

"Highly likely," he replied. "The most positive, most optimistic thing I can do is give them as much as I have and let them think for themselves."

"So?"

"So, Chautauqua."

Quinn took a drink of his Red Stripe and started to look at the menu.

Jodi gazed   at the boats in the marina. "This Ichabod's is definitely different than the other one."

Quinn nodded. "Yeah, and the food is much better. And a lot of cool characters at the bar." The waitress took their order and Quinn waved to a familiar face.

"There used to be a bar over on US 1, overlooking the river, *Durty Nelly's* – didn't stay open for too long, for some reason. Man, that was a pretty cool Irish pub, long before *Meg's* came along."

"Isn't there a *Durty Nelly's* in Boston?" she asked.

"Yeah, and in Gainesville. I recall sitting beside a gentleman there who had apparently been there on his stool a lot longer than I had. I was feeling rather down and I guess I did a lousy job hiding it."

"I've noticed that," Jodi quipped.

Quinn smiled. "After a while, he leaned over, put his hand on my shoulder and said with a smile, *No one wants to know.* 'Pardon?' I said with all the respect I could muster. The gentleman was well into his cup as the Irish say, and his voice was rough and raspy. *That's what the Devil told the teacher in Nashville.* I was at a loss. *Oh man, you haven't heard 'To Beat the Devil?'* On cue, he began to recite a poem Kris Kristofferson wrote about Johnny Cash. The end is great: *...now I ain't sayin I beat the Devil, but I drank his beer for nothing, then I stole his song.*

"Every time things get tough, I think of that song, because as Kristofferson says, *I don't believe that no one wants to know.* My brother-in-law taught me that song years before I ever taught a lesson," Quinn said.

"He was the gentleman?" Jodi asked.

"You've said more than you know, Ms. Richardson. Now there was a teacher. A pure teacher. He loved teaching. He loved learning. He was my mentor. Call him what you will. Pioneer. Trailblazer. Hardass. Rogue. But he has more integrity in the crack of his ...well, let's just say he has more integrity than anyone I've ever known. What did Hitchens say? You can't embrace the title of dissident unless you're willing to sacrifice. Hell, he wore it with a clear conscience. He was labeled, ostracized, persecuted, you name it and he'd never give an inch. Principals would threaten to fire him, transfer him, he wouldn't change. Shit, one of them came in during the summer and removed his podium, insisting he adopt some cooperative teaching method."

"What did he do?" asked Jodi

"Got his podium back, I'll tell you that."

"Tell me more," she said.

Quinn said, "One of these days I'm gonna write a book about him."

"Maybe you are already."

"He was the first to listen to me, like I knew what I was talking about. I didn't, of course, but he listened. That's an important trait in a teacher." Quinn raised his bottle to Jodi.

"My brother-in-law taught for over 45 years. They tried to honor him, and he would have none of it. He held up his hand like this—he has big old hands—smiled and said no thank you."

"Interesting man," said Jodi.

"Yeah, he knows Shakespeare better than anyone in the English department."

"Really?"

"Want to meet him? He's right over there."

Fresh Starts

Note to Tamara

I can't speak for anyone else, but no, the retirement thing is not a factor in my hard-headed refusal to give in. Actually, I see myself with the short-term memory of an NFL cornerback (a bad one). Although reflection is essential in this business, we have to shelve our struggles and frustrations pretty quickly. To thrive, we build upon our successes and walk away from our failures. Baseball taught me that. (there, two different sports references in one paragraph...is that some sort of a mixed metaphor?)

A mutual friend reminded me that our opportunity to start over each year — not from scratch — but again with a fresh start, is a true gift. You get another beginning!

> "Perhaps my best years are gone...but I wouldn't
> want them back. Not with the fire in me now."
> -Beckett

So after three decades, summer rolls on, and I begin to see August coming. I know I'm blessed with yet another chance to *get it right*...if only the candlesnuffers will leave me alone, I'll be fine. I started DROP last December and let me tell you, that was an agonizing decision. Financially, it was a no-brainer, but I can't tell you how many hours I fretted over the whole thing. What if they force me out before *I get it right?* Ha! That's what really got me writing, to tell you the truth.

As I said, I can't speak for anyone else...I sure hope I don't come off that way. A big part of my philosophy is the belief that each teacher must go down their own road. Collaboration has its limitations...maybe we shouldn't share everything we do in our classroom (hmmm...common core sacrilege). Hell, the great jazz cornet player, Buddy Bolden, used to cover his fingers with a handkerchief so no one could pick up his technique...maybe the best part of collaboration is finding out that each of us do have our own way.

The Fog of Idealism

The danger of doing too much preaching and not enough teaching is that it can lead to days when a teacher must come face to face with his own bullshit. Someone's usually around to help him trudge through it, and sometimes it's a student.

I spent many an evening sitting in the dark after 9/11. I wondered how it came to this. How did we go from being the most beloved nation in history in the summer of 1945 to this — in just over half a century? In the months following the attack, I remained glued to the television as if it were a window to the world, and I wondered if America the Idea wasn't the only thing left standing. I had always believed that America could be a force of good in the world. Maybe this would speed up the formulation of a coherent foreign policy that would be closer to who we are as a people; closer to our Creed. Could this possibly reawaken our sense of shared national purpose?

For much of my adult life, I had played the role of the devil's advocate. I schooled my students on the importance of the loyal opposition in a democracy. But I had grown weary of being the contrarian. I had often satisfied my libertarian urges by being on *the wrong side* of the things, but it had grown tiresome.

In 2003, the Bush Administration was building a case for intervention in Iraq and I was all ears. I wanted my country to be right. I wanted my president to be right. I rooted for him like I root for my beloved Gators and Steelers — with blind passion.

There actually was a pretty solid argument for intervention, and I gathered my points. We had a long history with Saddam Hussein, dating back to 1968. Saddam and his Baath Party had come to power with the help of a CIA coup. He had engaged in an extermination campaign in the northern provinces. There was evidence of war crimes committed during the war with Iran. In his UN speech, President Bush gave his own reasons: *the refusal of Saddam to come into compliance concerning Weapons of Mass Destruction; and the involvement of Baathists in Islamic terror groups.*

I grew frustrated with the arguments against intervention. I couldn't help but ask myself if some were protesting the war purely for the sake of dissenting? When did persecution and ostracism became badges of validation? I saw the opposition to action as a symptom of deeper problems in America and I couldn't get out of my own way. I began to write an editorial:

> *The innocence of youth is gone, but idealism returns like the spring. It is tempered by a century which taught us that blind faith is not patriotism, and blind pacifism is not righteousness. It is self-righteousness. I am just a school teacher, but I know which way the wind blows...*

What really happened was my idealism went haywire. I sounded like a neo-con right out of the West Wing. "Is it possible to have economic and political interests and still be morally upright?" "Do mixed motives taint the righteousness of a cause?" Bleh!

I held Bush's feet to the fire, saying, "He knows the blood of this war is on his hands." But I spent more time attacking the opposition than listening to them. Rather than having a nice sit-down debate, I hit them with all sorts of philosophical bullshit. I hammered them from above:

> *The war on terrorism is not simply a struggle to preserve our well-being. It is, in fact, another chapter in a long fight to rid the world of threats to the very essence of the human condition. We are united **not** by ethnic or religious bonds, but by a political culture. That culture is founded on the rights of individuals and the responsibilities of those individuals to free others. Liberty is not a legal matter, but a moral one.*

Not only was I flowing with righteousness, I was standing in the slop. To be sure, I was annoyed by what I saw as blind dissent. Just because you opposed the administration's economic, environmental and education policies didn't mean you had to oppose its foreign policy:

> *Just because oil was a factor shouldn't contaminate other reasons for intervention in Iraq. Must we condemn all political action because it is tainted by economic interests? Be wary of any morality based on the resentment of the rich and powerful. It is too easy to judge a man or a*

> *nation by seeing all power and wealth as evil. Am I bound to think only within the constraints of an ideology? If I have disagreements with President Bush over domestic policies, must I oppose all actions of his administration? The last time I checked, that's not liberalism. It's dogma.*

I wasn't done:

> *To the blind dissenter, we are the vast huddle of sleepy consumers, following a hypocritical government. American foreign policy is attacked as being selective. Within some warped perception of consistency, we are compelled to either free everyone, or free no one. Heaven help you if you're stuck in a life boat with someone from that school of thought. Can we slay all the dragons? No, but should that deter us from doing what we can? I am reminded of Edmund Burke, who said that the greatest mistake is to do nothing.*

Then I began a series of correspondences with a former student who I had grown to respect during his time in my class. He sent me a picture showing his participation in a peaceful protest against military action in Iraq. Randy was taking it to the streets, marching for what he believed in — doing what I had tirelessly talked about in class. He was a free thinking citizen, taking public action.

Instead of responding as a proud teacher, I fired off a volley of arguments that must have made him think I had been kidnapped and brainwashed. Not only had I switched positions, my responses to his points were arrogant and aloof. Rather than presenting sound reasons — and there were several — for military action in Iraq, I reacted with naïve` self-righteous crap. I missed the chance at having a much-coveted debate on American foreign policy because I was too busy preaching. Somehow, Randy overlooked my bombast and responded with civil, thoughtful points.

The memory of this exchange has endured for over a decade. It bothers me to this day. I finally came around and realized that my fear and anger over 9/11 had skewed my judgment. But it was not so much the side I took in the debate that bothers me. It was the way in which I argued that was a betrayal of what I had long stood for. I attacked those who disagreed with me. Jefferson believed that reason is the convergence of thought and emotion, and I forgot the "thought" part. I am thankful that what came out of this was a strong friendship.

Sometimes, the student is the teacher. This one taught me a lesson I'll not soon forget. Thank you Randy Browne.

Through all of this, I have to say that the mess made by the Iraq War clouds its legitimacy. Had we been able to establish a stable state in Iraq, would the purpose of the war be seen with more credibility? I am reminded of Nikita Khrushchev's comments on the American foray into Cuba (Bay of Pigs). He said our only mistake was failing. As you can see, my skepticism has returned and is alive and well.

June 6th

Quinn saw there was a new text on his phone.

Jodi: hey, it's Jodi. How's your summer going?

Quinn: Good. How are you?

Jodi: Not terrible. How long did it take you to type that? (Smiling)

Quinn: took the dogs to the beach yesterday…water was coke bottle green

Jodi: Ha! dogs on the beach? Isn't that illegal?

Quinn: It's immoral not to take 'em…(smiling).

Jodi: Reading your stuff…enjoying some of it

Quinn: feedback?

Jodi: I'm off for the summer. Remember?

Storied

"Such as she was, such as she would become."
-Robert Frost

On my bookshelf sits a coffee cup. Inside it there is a small blue and gold kaleidoscope, given to me by a student. When she graduated, she presented me with this gift, thanking me for helping her see things a little differently. It is a prized possession. More times than you can know, I glance back at the kaleidoscope as a reminder. Sarah's gift holds me to my obligation to both my subject and my students.

I have spoken often of the importance of a teacher loving his subject, but something would be missing if I didn't talk about those sitting right in front of me. The connection that I build with a student is essential to both of us succeeding. I have been blessed by the ability to see more in them than they sometimes see in themselves--just as my mentors saw more in me. It often makes me impatient, intolerant, and unreasonable with their youth. I anger easily but I forgive easily. My withering rants and blistering sermons quickly melt away with the sound of laughter or a warm greeting.

Years later, when I receive a letter, an email, a graduation announcement, or a wedding invitation, it is rewarding beyond words.

When I speak of my former students, I talk with my hat in my hand. So many of them are living out American dreams. So many are trying to make the world around them a better place to be. It's not a straight line for most, nor was it for me. But I heard Maya Angelou say once that it was impossible to be successful in anything without making those around you successful. Many have done just that.

For over thirty years, young people filed into stuffy rooms and sat on uncomfortable furniture listening to my stories. Oh, how I do love to hear theirs. Who are these young men and women? Where did they go and what did they become? When once they were unknowing; bemused , they are now storied.

"So, what are you going to be, anyway?" I asked the quiet girl with salt water in her ears. "I am going to be a spy," she replied, with all the confidence she could muster. Years later, the suits showed up at school to do a background check for her security clearance, and things got interesting.

When she graduated high school, Corynn left her beloved beach town and headed to Gainesville, earning a B.A. in Russian and Political Science from the University of Florida, and then an M.A. in National Security from Georgetown.

Corynn didn't go the spy route. Instead, she's a Special Agent with the Bureau of Diplomatic Security within the Department of State. She began her career as a federal agent at the New York Field Office running protective details for two Secretaries of State, the Dalai Lama and Prince Charles.

She went on to work on counterintelligence issues for the Department in Beijing, China, then served several years in both India and Algeria. Corynn responded to the Mumbai terrorist attacks in 2008 where six Americans were killed. She was the first US federal law enforcement officer on site and was later awarded the *Women in Federal Law Enforcement's Julie Y. Cross Award* for her role in the response and subsequent investigation of the attacks.

During her assignment to the US Embassy in Algiers, she was part of the first team assigned temporary duty to Tunis, Tunisia at the onset of the Arab Spring in 2011 and worked to protect the Mission there from hostile elements on the ground. She then served as Regional Security Officer in Bamako, Mali. During her tenure there, Corynn led the Embassy's security program through a coup d'état, a French-led military intervention, and an Ebola crisis.

Corynn is currently assigned to the National Joint Terrorism Task Force as a liaison officer for the State Department. She is married to a fellow Floridian, who also serves the Department at embassies abroad. They have three beagles with international passports, and a dream home in Melbourne Beach where they look forward to eventual retirement.

There are others, you know. Thousands.

One is an architect living in China, the country of her birth; there's a Captain in the United States Air Force; a lead singer in a band; the owner of a hardware store; a surgeon in a Brooklyn emergency room.

There are mothers and fathers; fire fighters and police officers; United States Marines; baseball, football, soccer, and golf coaches; graduates of the Naval Academy and West Point.

Another is a lawyer for victims of human trafficking... and then there's the professional surfer; a physician who volunteered in a small town in Appalachia; and the only skateboarding Professor of History in America. Some are teachers that work right alongside me —one an Army veteran who earned his Masters and PhD, but still teaches high school kids right down the hall. And then there's that saxophone player, traveling the country playing in Jazz clubs.

Others are in medical school and law school; an Australian kid is writing his dissertation on the politics of Scotland; one is a DNA crime lab analyst who may love baseball more than I do.

There are engineers, finance managers, judicial clerks, preachers, college athletes, and artists--one who lives deep in the Maine woods. A former professional baseball player moved back home to raise a family and teach the game to teenagers. There's an art teacher who volunteered to teach in Ecuador and spent five years learning Spanish so she could.

One is a global health activist; a country music DJ; an announcer for a National Hockey League team; there are magazine and newspaper editors; English teachers and writers who have returned to lead me through this wilderness. Some are adoptive parents; environmental activists; pro football players. One's a brick mason, another is an antique furniture collector.

There's a Navy and Merchant Marine veteran; there are postal workers, librarians, nonprofit fundraisers… a veterinarian who studied on St. Kitts in the Caribbean, an orthopedic foot and ankle physician, and a pilot who once used my Woody Guthrie story to get a date.

One is a lawyer who works out of her home so she can be with her kids…there's a bartender, a ballet dancer, a nurse practitioner, and a volunteer at the Early Intervention Center. Another gave up the teaching profession to become the youth director at his church.

Many of them have their pictures on the wall. Oh, did I mention *the wall*? It's a massive collage of hundreds of students' faces, amongst family, friends, and other favorite people. It all started about fifteen years ago when the roof leaked, and I had a bunch of damaged drywall. I needed to cover it somehow, and as time passed, the wall took on a life of its own.

All tangled up with an inordinate number of pictures of dogs and grandchildren hang artifacts and treasures from once and former students. There's a piece of birch bark brought to me by a girl from her New England vacation. She's a nurse now, and a triathlete, living in south Florida. She used to bring me lunch now and then during her college days. One meal she brought to school included a cool beverage, but that's another story. There's a T-shirt and a pair of batting gloves hanging up there, and a painting of Hemingway, brought to me from Cuba by my favorite Auburn Tiger. She also brought me a box of cigars on her return from her church mission. They were taken by Customs, but somehow she showed up in Melbourne with one, and I was obliged to destroy the evidence, slowly, very slowly.

There's Tom Petty, Alice Paul, and Marcus Garvey; Bob Dylan and Thomas Jefferson are up there, with Buddy Holly, and 9/11 firefighters; Barry Goldwater and Elvis Costello; Jacqueline Kennedy, Muddy Waters, and a *Save the Everglades* poster.

John Wayne's up there, along with Cesar Chavez, Carl Hiaasen, and Ray Charles. Don't forget the Rolling Stones; Susan B. Anthony, Bob Marley, A. Bartlett Giamatti, and Joan Baez.

Then there is Gandhi, Dave Matthews, and Hillary Clinton. Bruce Springsteen is on there, and a Pittsburgh Steeler bumper sticker; and how about Woody Guthrie and Dwight Eisenhower; ML King and RE Lee and Tim Tebow; Einstein, Denzel Washington, Robert Duvall, Willie Nelson, Che Guevera, and Malcolm X.

Mostly, there are students — scholars, athletes, debutantes, and Eagle Scouts. They are now surgeons, soldiers, pastors, and fishermen; auto mechanics, psychologists, and physical therapists; authors of children's books and yoga instructors.

I have a mantra — I'm not even sure where I got it---I've been saying it so long I can't remember: "The spirit of liberty doesn't imply that each person will do great things, only that he or she will do their own things." Not all the stories have happy endings. There are divorces and bankruptcies and incarcerations. And there have been far too many losses of those serving in the military. Still, I'm humbled by their achievements and inspired by their resilience.

The right to pursue happiness is a mystifying proposition. It's the essential phrase in Jefferson's work, for if that chase is waged with integrity and accountability, then we all benefit in some way from each other's pursuits.

I try to keep up with as many former students as I can. Email and Facebook have been blessings when it comes to staying in touch. Yes, there are countless flaws with the social media. Plenty of narcissism and superficiality to go around. But on the other hand, such networks are windows into people's lives. If we look closely at the flashes of life, it can affirm so much of Jefferson's claim that free people make the best of all possible worlds.

August 5

Monday, Monday. Can't trust that day. It was Thursday, but the song was stuck in his head. Quinn filed into the cafeteria with his colleagues. Second day back after a nice long summer. All he could think about was the conversation he had with his brother in law the day before:

"How come you never had that *Mr. Smith goes to Washington* moment?"

"Why didn't I snap?"

"Yeah, just blow up at a faculty meeting..."

"Because I didn't give a damn what other people thought," Ted answered.

"So, what if I did that?" Quinn asked, "You think I'd be just trying to go out in a blaze of glory?"

"Frank, you can only control what you can control. Trying to rile a teacher is like kicking a cow in the ass." Ted was the ultimate individualist. He got no satisfaction out of rallying the troops. The itch to lead a revolt did not afflict him.

Quinn on the other hand, had a steel mill labor union agitator in his blood. Ray had hit the nail on the head when he accused Quinn of wanting to go down in flames. Maybe he did. "So if I storm up to the front and give some *I'm mad as hell and I'm not gonna take it anymore* rant, you think it's just my vanity talking?"

"I didn't say that Francis."

Quinn looked up and saw yet another slide show beginning. He checked the baseball scores on his phone and then scrolled through his messages. He reread last night's conversation with his son:

Tim: I work till 9. Will you be home?

Quinn: Yeah. Just had a great talk with your uncle. Advised me not to burn the house down!

Quinn: Should have learned that already from the time I went after the union leader (mistake). Standing up against this stuff is risky, especially for the young ones. Not sure if anyone wants to stick his neck out these days—not sure I blame them. I can't be a fool.

Tim: and I can't help but continuously tell you to go where you are valued. That place doesn't value you. Why give them an ounce of your talent?

Quinn: I was born to be a teacher. That's what God made me to do. Not sure where value comes in.

Tim: I guess I'm confused on what the issue is, are you just miserable because you feel like you can't be a good teacher there?

Quinn: Misery. Splendid misery.

Tim: At work. Call you in a bit

(Quinn kept on texting)

Quinn: I love teaching. My own profession is going to shit. Make no mistake, I'll fight the fight. I'll do what I want in class, but should I make a stand? What do I owe the profession?

Tim: not an effing thing, dad

Quinn: What I was trying to say is, do I have an obligation to speak up? To make that last stand at the faculty meeting? Your uncle said no. he said "just do what you do in your classroom." Then when I was leaving, he said, "Francis, you need to do what you need to do." Whatever that means.

Tim: Ha! it means you should stand up and go off—Stand up for what you believe in or what's gonna happen to all those numb-nuts who will be teaching my kids?

Quinn: My own son calling me out. Voltaire said tend to your own garden…don't try to save the world

Tim: Well

Quinn: I'll just let the spirit move me. Maybe I'll finish the book first

Tim: yeah lol

Quinn had rehearsed the diatribe for years while mowing the grass. He thought of exactly what he'd say; and he hoped he wouldn't start cussing, although all of this was profane. He knew what would set him off. He could see himself doing this, but Ray's voice was in his ear: "If you don't think you can change things, then why in the hell would you do it? Self-satisfaction? You wanna feel all righteous?"

The meeting dragged on. Countless slides on a power point. Black and White. Just bullets, no clip art even. In the midst of a mind-numbing presentation on lesson plan design, Quinn let his mind drift. He envisioned himself in front of a new group of sophomores. He thought about a lesson one week in — *the Road to Revolution*. But   this day was playing too close to the script and he could feel himself twitch. The   first half of the meeting was filled with promises about protecting teacher autonomy. The second half dealt with all the standardization requirements — the proverbial pissing on your foot and telling you it's raining.

Finally he stood up. "I've had enough," he said as he walked right down the center aisle. When he got to the front, he paused and said again in a low voice, "I've had enough," and then moved toward the door. Just before he reached the exit, he stopped, stood for a moment, then turned. He stared at the crowd of teachers and administrators. Quinn smiled and turned back toward the door and walked out. He kept on walking.

He made his way to the green bench and there he sat. It was halfway in the shade so the heat was bearable. Quinn didn't seem to care. Just then his phone vibrated.

Jodi: Did you see the moon this morning, Mr. Quinn?

Waning Gibbous. Straight overhead at first light. The sky was clear, just a hint of blue.

Gotta be a noticer, Quinn

Quinn smiled. Again he thought about that new batch of sophomores coming.

August 8

Quinn remembered reading that Carl Hiaasen was speaking at a bookstore in Vero Beach, and he couldn't miss it. He apologized to the dogs for leaving them behind and then drove south. It was a hot August Saturday…Quinn drove his truck with the windows down and the air conditioner on. He took A1A down as far as he could, listening to a homemade Buffett CD on the way.

The place was filled to capacity and Hiaasen didn't disappoint. He spoke with great humor about very serious things. Quinn waited patiently afterward to meet his fellow Floridian and have a book signed for his nephew. Upon shaking his hand, he told Hiaasen how he cited the author often in his history classes… Hiaasen was a bit taken aback. He was humble, gracious, and of course, funny: "I'm both flattered and terrified."

When Quinn checked his phone after getting back in his truck, he saw that there was a baseball update and a text from Jodi:

Where are you? In labor 6 hrs. now…

It was late afternoon. Quinn drove straight to Holmes Regional from Vero and parked on the east side. He crossed the street but stopped before he went in and looked up at the sprawling building. "Some of the happiest and saddest days were spent here," he thought. He went into the lobby, sat down and waited.

Quinn sat alone in the waiting room trying to ignore the local news on the TV, and making small talk with the security guard at the desk. He called his daughter and asked her to go let out the dogs and feed them.

Finally, a girl he didn't recognize came out into the lobby. She walked over and asked, "Are you Mr. Quinn?"

"Yes," he replied, standing up.

"I'm Jamie, Jodi's sister."

"Pleased to meet you," Quinn said, shaking her hand.

"It's a girl; eight pounds, six ounces…everything's okay…my mom is up there with her," Jamie said.

"Stella," he said.

"Yeah, Stella." Jamie said, smiling. "Thank you for being here,"

"Well, thank you for letting me know. Tell me," Quinn asked, "how'd she know I was here?"

"She knew." Jamie shrugged and smiled again. "Are you coming back tomorrow?" she asked. "I'm sure she'd like to see you."

Quinn assured her he would, then turned and headed for the elevator. He crossed the street to the parking lot, climbed into his truck and pulled onto Hickory Street. He turned on Hibiscus and headed toward home. The colors of the sunset spread like wildfire across the western sky.

Rootholds

Won't you disregard the feeling that I have been so scarred
From enduring the works of a certain English bard.
But there was seldom something to sink my teeth into.
And the stuff of Eliot and Conrad and Camus
Can lead a man to stare up at the ceiling
And slump down in the pew.
Indeed my old professors would like to have me tarred
For openly admitting that I learned more of truth
Just from sitting around the barbeque
In my brother-in-law's back yard.

In barbershops, at bus stops,
And exchanges over countertops,
It's the wisdom of the commonplace, I've found.
From smoky tavern conversations to park bench visitations
With lonely folks downtown—flesh and bone—
living out their lives alone.
You can't find it all written down,
For the truth ain't always leather bound.

Please don't misunderstand me;
That the classics should be tossed.
Me, I cut my teeth on Sandburg, Twain, and Frost.
And sometimes I like to sit outside in the remnants of a day
Chewing on the words of Ernest Hemingway.

But we steep ourselves with knowledge
Then we stand right in the slop.
And sophisticate ourselves until our eyes are crossed!
We place the burden on our shoulders
To wander till we drop,
Searching for a meaning that we lost. (sigh)

So come on by and sit awhile,
We'll talk of things that make us smile.
There's a breeze across the porch today,
I'll open up a couple beers

And put on some vinyl records we haven't heard in years.

So let the stories flow;
Of Williams and DiMaggio…
Of kids and dogs, of oaks and palms,
And orange moons rising.
Of tire swings and wedding rings
And the lonely song the highway sings.
These are the musings of a common man.
…his rootholds.
Flesh and bone…finding meaning on his own…

So Much To Be Done...

Years ago, I took a line from a Jimmy Buffett song (*Last Mango...*) and stuck it on my door: "There's still so much to be done." Like so many things, it served not only to remind my students, but also to remind me, that there are a thousand more things to think about; to talk about; to do.

As I leaf through these pages, I realize that there are a thousand more things to say. But this is what I have, for now.

When I hear my friends and colleagues talk about retirement and leaving this profession, I can't fathom it. It's hard for me to imagine not doing this. There will in fact be a day when I leave the classroom, but I ain't leaving yet.

I heard a writer once say that teaching was bad for his craft because it sucked him dry of emotion and intellectual energy. I'm not sure I understand. Students can give much more than they ever take away. What wears us down as teachers is the fight we wage just to do what we love to do. But since loving something is the only rational act, we just keep doing it.

It is Sunday morning on the back porch — my cathedral. It's October again, and the temperature has slipped into the sixties. A change of seasons in Florida. The sun is coming up through the trees, and as I sit here amongst the artifacts, with the dogs at my feet, I think about the promise the day brings. Yeah, Jimmy, there's still so much to be done.

References

Bellah, Robert N., Richard Madsen, William M. Sullivan, Ann Swidler, and Steven M. Tipton. *Habits of the Heart, Individualism and Commitment in American Life.* Berkeley: University of California Press, 1985.

Claiborne, Shane. *The Irresistible Revolution: Living as an Ordinary Radical.* Grand Rapids: Zondervan, 2006.

Dallek, Robert. *An Unfinished Life, John F. Kennedy 1917-1963.* New York: Little Brown and Company, 2003.

Dylan, Bob. *Chronicles, Volume One.* New York: Simon and Schuster, 2004.

Foote, Shelby. "The Art of Fiction No. 15" *The Paris Review, Summer 1999.* http://www.theparisreview.org/interviews/931/the-art-of-fiction-no-158-shelby-foote

Frost, Robert. *The Poetry of Robert Frost.* Edward Connery Latham, editor. New York: Holt, Rinehart, and Winston, 1969.

Gould, Lewis L. August 2008. *Return of the Roughrider.* Smithsonian Magazine (August 2008): http://www.smithsonianmag.com/history/1912-republican-convention-855607/?no-ist.

Greenstein, Fred I., "Nine Presidents in Search of a Modern Presidency." Fred Greenstein, editor. *Leadership in the Modern Presidency.* Cambridge, MA: President and Fellows of Harvard College, 1988.

Hemingway, Ernest. *The Complete Short Stories of Ernest Hemingway.* New York: Charles Scribner's Sons/MacMillan Publishing Company, 1987.

Hemingway, Ernest. *A Moveable Feast.* New York: Touchstone, 1992.

Kateb, George, *Democratic Individuality and the Meaning of Rights*
Nancy L. Rosenblum, editor. *Liberalism and the Moral Life*. Cambridge:
Harvard University Press, 1989.

Kennedy, John F. *Remarks at Amherst College,* October 26, 1963.
Retrieved from http://arts.gov/about/kennedy.

Kernell, Samuel. *Going Public*. Washington D.C.: CQ Press, 1986.

Kymlicka, Will. *Contemporary Political Philosophy-An Introduction*.
Oxford: Clarendon Press, 1990.

Lerner, Max. *Tocqueville and American Civilization*. New York: Harper
and Row, Publishers, Inc., 1966.

Leuchtenburg, William E., "Franklin D. Roosevelt: The First Modern
President," Fred I. Greenstein, editor. *Leadership in the Modern
Presidency*. Cambridge: President and Fellows of Harvard College,
1988.

Marsalis, Wynton. September 12, 2005. "Saving America's Soul
Kitchen" *TIME Magazine*, Vol. 166 No. 11.

May, Gita. "Tocqueville and the Enlightenment Legacy," Abraham
Eisenstadt, editor. *Reconsidering Tocqueville's Democracy in America*.
New Brunswick: Rutgers University Press, 1988.

McClosky, Herbert and John Zaller. *The American Ethos*. Cambridge:
Harvard University Press, 1984.

Mill, John Stuart. *De Tocqueville on Democracy in America, I.* London
Review. October 1835.

Monrone, James A. *The Democratic Wish, Popular Participation and the
Limits of American Government.* New York: BasicBooks, 1990.

Morley, Jefferson. "Darkness on the Edge of the Shining City" *New
Republic*. Vol 196, Number 12, Issue 3, 766, March 23, 1987.

Muir, William K., Jr., "Ronald Reagan: The Primacy of Rhetoric."
Fred Greenstein, editor. *Leadership in the Modern Presidency*.
Cambridge, MA: President and Fellows of Harvard College, 1988.

Needleman, Jacob. *The American Soul, Rediscovering the Wisdom of the Founders*. New York: Penguin Putnam Inc., 2002.

Reeves, Richard. *President Kennedy, Profile of Power*. New York: Touchstone, 1993.

Sandburg, Carl. *Abraham Lincoln, The Prairie Years 2* (New York: Harcourt Brace and Company, 1926.

Schambra, William A. August 2012. *The Origins and Revival of Constitutional Conservatism: 1912 and 2012*. First Principles. Washington DC: Heritage Foundation. http://www. Heritage.org/research.org/research/reports/2012/08/the-origins-and-revival-of-constitutional- conservatism-1912-and- 2012.

Schlesinger, Arthur, Jr., "Individualism and Apathy in Tocqueville's Democracy," Abraham Eisenstadt, editor. 1988. *Reconsidering Tocqueville's Democracy in America*. New Brunswick: Rutgers University Press, 1988.

Schiefer, Bob and Gary Paul Gates. *The Acting President*. New York: E.P. Dutton, 1989.

Stegner, Wallace. *Sense of Place*. New York: Random House, Inc., 1992. Retrieved from http://www.pugetsound.edu/files/resources/7040_Stegner,%20Wallace%20%20Sense%20of%20Place.pdf.

Stockman, David A. *The Triumph of Politics, Why the Reagan Revolution Failed*. New York: Harper and Row, 1986.

Sullivan, Andrew. "Mr. Average" *The New Republic*. Vol. 200, Numbers 2 & 3, Issues 3860 & 3861, January 9 and 16, 1989.

Bolte Taylor, Jill. *My Stroke of Insight: A Brain Scientist's Personal Journey*. Viking, 2008.

The Poetry Foundation.
http://www.poetryfoundation.org/bio/robert-frost

Tocqueville, Alexis de (George Lawrence translation). 1835, 1840. Democracy in America. J.P. Mayer, editor. New York: Harper and Row 1969.

Travis, Clay. *On the Confederate Flag.* http://www.foxsports.com/college-football/outkick-the-coverage/on-the-confederate-flag-062415 (June 24, 2015).

Wattenberg, Martin P. "From a Partisan to a Candidate-Centered Electorate," Anthony King, editor. *The New American Political System.* Second Version. Washington D.C.: The AEI Press, 1990.

Wildavsky, Aaron, "A World of Difference--The Public Philosophies and Political Behaviors of Rival American Cultures," Anthony King, editor. *The New American Political System.* Second Version. Washington D.C. The AEI Press, 1990.

Wills, Garry. *Lincoln at Gettysburg, The Words that Remade America.* New York: Simon and Schuster, 1992.

Wills, Garry. *Inventing America, Jefferson's Declaration of Independence.* New York: Houghton Mifflin, 2002.

Yarbrough, Jean. *Theodore Roosevelt and the American Political Tradition,* Lawrence: University Press of Kansas, 2012.

Zetterbaum, Marvin. *Tocqueville and the Problem of Democracy.* Stanford: Stanford University Press, 1967.

46000747R00161

Made in the USA
Lexington, KY
19 October 2015